I'll Sing Again Tomorrow

A Memoir

I'll Sing Again Tomorrow

A Memoir

Rene Terry Mucci

Copyright © 2022 by Rene Terry Mucci
All rights reserved.

This book, or parts thereof, may not be reproduced in any form
without prior written permission of the publisher.

Published by Sarnaylah Press
Boston, Massachusetts

Front cover, author, and most interior photos
courtesy of Rene Terry Mucci. Sparrow photo by Lee of Adobe Stock.

Various photos of Moma courtesy of Gerardine Mendez, Wansaifla Geffrard,
Anita Edwards, Amanda Rich, Shorna Dyer, Gigi Elabbar,
and all others—you know who you are!

Interior book design by Mi Ae Lipe (whatnowdesign.com).
Front cover design by Anna Burrous and Mi Ae Lipe.

Printed in the United States of America.

To contact the author or order additional copies:
ReneTerryMucci@gmail.com
ReneTerryMucci.com

First Edition, 2022
Print ISBN: 978-0-578-94369-5
Ebook ISBN: 978-0-578-66636-5
Library of Congress Control Number: 2021913088

*This saga is dedicated to Moma,
who is sharing her dance with me,
and my husband, John, who is my Big Italian Meatball.*

*Thank you for lifting my head above water,
keeping my feet on the ground,
holding me together for today and
helping me believe in a better tomorrow.*

Without you, I am never whole.

*Life is full of joy and tears.
Lots of surprises,
Winding roads of sunlit trees…
or maybe snow-covered treetops.*

Ever changing. Often bumpy. Sometimes slippery.

*Hold on with both hands…
pray for guidance and smile.
Find happiness in everything.*

Contents

Acknowledgments	xiv
Angels Earning Wings	xv
Preface	xvi

PART 1 — THE JOURNEY BEGINS...	**1**
Beginning Something New	2
No Mistakes	6
Betsy	8
The Dance	9
Hello, Walmart	10
Nayla	12
Routine	14
Thoughts	16
Granny's Ways	17
Simple Things	19
Chocolate	20

PART 2 — KEEPING IT REAL	**21**
Life Keeps Going	22
Viewpoints	23
Moma's Birthday	24
Just Life	25
Changes	26
Life's Lists	27
Shake It Off	28
Small Is Small	29
Trust	30

PART 3 — RAINY DAYS AND PERIWINKLES 31
A Day in May 32
Quintessential 33
Circles and Swirls 34
Peaks and Valleys 36
How Lucky Are We? 37
The Path Beyond 38
Caregiver 40
Story of Life 41

PART 4 — LIVING LIFE 43
Enjoy Simple Pleasures 44
Life's Puzzles 45
Supposed to Be 46
Circle of Prayer 47
Good Talk 48

PART 5 — BE STILL 49
Be Still and Know 50
Moma's Round Table 51
Treasures from Home 52
Last Box 53

PART 6 — MAKING EVERY DAY COUNT 55
Lead or Follow—Just Keep Going 56
Making a Difference 57
Jeans 58
Retirement 59
One on One 60
Moma's Birthday 61

PART 7 — BREATHE AND FEEL BLESSED 63
Interpretation 64
Vulnerability 66

Moma's Tree	67
Sharing Clouds	69
Birthday Month	70
50–50	71

PART 8 — ROAD TRIP   **73**

Life's Surprise	74
The Drive Begins	75
Florida Orange Juice	76
It's "Me," Moma	77
Our Visit	79
One Step at a Time	80
Our Time Together	81
Doctor Visit	82
Assistance	84
Safety Lock	85
Rather Be Known—Than Remembered	86
Leaving to Return	88
Our Rainbow	90
Wonderful	91

PART 9 — BACK IN RHYTHM   **93**

Lesson Learned	94
What to Do with Keys	96
Silver Alert	97
Mind's Eye	98
Dementia in the Forefront	99

PART 10 — LIFE IS ALL THINGS   **101**

24-Hour Day	102
Loving Both	103
The Question	104
Calamine Lotion	105
Presidential Speech	106
Tiny Sparrow	107

PART 11 — THANKFULNESS	**109**
Partners	110
Coins	111
Quarter Pound	112
PART 12 — TIME OF WHIRLWIND	**113**
The Fall	114
Nights at JFK Hospital	116
Transfer	118
Recovery Begins	119
Dark Days	120
Moma's Bed	122
Happy Heart	124
Are You MY Rene?	125
Homeward Bound	127
The Reunion	128
March 10, 1930, Birthdate	129
Slippery Slope	130
"In the Neighborhood"	132
Good Moments	133
John's Arms	134
PART 13 — MOVING ON	**135**
New Chapter of Life	136
"Doctor's" Orders	137
Something Good	138
Monday, Wednesday, Friday	140
Hiding "Mistakes"	141
Embrace the Bumps	142
Losing Yourself	144
PART 14 — DEAR GOD	**145**
I'll Be Waiting	146
Moments of Memory	147

Hurting	148
Hell	149
Two Potted Trees	150
New Moves	152
Misplaced Past	153
PART 15 — LIFE IS…	**155**
Heaven	156
The Search	157
Life Is	158
Fractured Fairy Tale	159
Fafa	160
Surely Joy Remains	162
Moma's Reality	163
PART 16 — TRUSTING	**165**
News of the Day	166
Allowances for God	167
The Eve of Past Extremes	169
PART 17 — SLIPPING THROUGH TIME	**171**
Moma's Birthday	172
"Present"	173
Present, Past Time	174
Mother's Day	175
Four-Foot Teddy Bear	176
My "Present"	178
PART 18 — LIFE WITH HARD EDGES	**179**
Rerun	180
Two-Hand Rule	181
Spiraling	182
ID	183
God Is in the Driver's Seat	184

The Love Word 185
Moma's Tree Revisited 186
Find the Words 187

PART 19 — PROMISE ME ALWAYS **189**
Always 190
Her World 192
Robert…Robert 193
Never Let Go 194
My Prayer to God 195
Memory Sign 196
Atwaba 197
I'm Me 198
Moma's Birthday 199

**PART 20 — BALANCING ON
STEPPING-STONES** **201**
Navigating Through Thorns 202
Beginning New Routine 203
Candlelight 205
Memory Connection 206
Remember to Remember 207

**PART 21 — FLOWERS STILL BLOOM,
BIRDS STILL SING** **209**
Pure Magic 210
Angel Prayers 211
Joining in Heaven 212
Dream 214
Remember the Flowers and Birds 215
A Year Ago, a Year from Now 216

PART 22 — SELF-JOURNEY **217**
Your Self-Journey 218
51–49 219

Revolving Door 220
Shared History 221
God's Dance 222
30-Minute Visit with God 223
Snapshot of Us 224
I Received a Call 226

**PART 23 — PUZZLE PIECES
ON THE FLOOR** **227**
Moma's Birthday 228
Emotions and Actions 229
Puzzle 230
Conversation with Daddy 231

PART 24 — OUR NEW JOURNEY BEGINS **233**
New Reality 234
24-Hour Care 235
Smooth as Peanut Butter 236
New Surroundings 238
Dinnertime 239
Teeth, Anyone? 241
New Life 242
Our Angel, Nayla 244
Intuition 246

PART 25 — LIFE MOVING ON **249**
Closer to Heaven 250
Settling In 251
Feeling of Happiness 252
Know You Will Be Okay 253

PART 26 — HOMEWARD BOUND **255**
God Has Taken Over 256
Sarah 258
I Love You Forever 260

Acknowledgments

"It takes a village." This proverb has been borrowed so many times—this is once more.

You see, while being Moma's caregiver, we were surrounded by so many wonderful people. Her doctor and nurses followed her medical needs. Her caregivers were there for our daily needs. Her friends were always nearby to lend a hand. My husband John picked us up every time we fell.

And God, He carried us through it all.

With humble gratitude—thank you.

Angels Earning Wings

It takes a special kind of person to be a caregiver. It's not just caring for someone but rather putting yourself in their shoes to help them with their journey. It takes an angel earning their wings.

> Gerardine Mendez
> Wansaifla Geffrard
> Anita Edwards
> Amanda Rich
> Shorna Dyer
> Gigi Elabbar
>
> and all others—you know who you are!

For the wonderfully talented women who helped bring Moma's and my journey to life in book form—my full gratitude is yours.
   Thank you.

> Lynn Post
> Anna Burrous
> Mi Ae Lipe

Preface

Everyone's journey is different. Personal "life" never leaves your mind completely and will shape the memories that are left you along the way. This is the road traveled by Moma and me, in our journey together.

It's been ten years since Moma's diagnosis of dementia. It was slow progression at first. I believe it was God's way of allowing me to catch up and prepare for the inevitable. I can say, without any hesitation, these ten years were the worst time in my life ~ feeling helpless to Moma's disease. However, it has also been the most rewarding to be her caregiver and hold her hand when she didn't know me, but smiled at me anyway.

This is Moma's and my journey... a day in the life of dementia.
Balancing on stepping-stones,
maneuvering through thorns,
therapy in motion.

Moma with her Nayla.

Part 1
The Journey Begins...

Diagnosis early 2009
Began book 2013
February 7, 2013 – March 2013

Life—be kind to me.
My memories are fading.
Yesterdays flow into today,
leaving tomorrow a mystery.

Thoughts scatter from the corners of my mind
and vanish as quickly as they appear.

I sometimes fail to know you,
but I will always love who you are to me
and the way you make me feel.

Beginning Something New

The journey begins. Small changes at first... forgotten dates. Missed reminders. Always with good excuses that I believed. I wanted to. I needed to.

Then the diagnosis comes, "Your mom has the beginnings of dementia." She's 80... it's normal, I say to myself. To be expected. Really.

And then the denial begins. "Stay focused, Moma." Write it down, Moma. Post a calendar and mark off the days. Surely, this will help. No? Then let me do it for you.

And soon to follow comes, "You're not letting me be the Moma!" The struggle to remain independent has begun. Each day brings something new. Quick... start reading. Study hard. There MUST be something I can do! And this was my mind site. This too can be "fixed." Not far from the truth, only it was me, I, who needed the fixing! The mere fact that I thought I could control the situation shows that I was out of control. So began the trial and error period. Panic came to mind a lot due to uncertainty of our next step...

Let's take a peek into Moma's mind for a moment. Fully aware of changes happening within her, but not knowing what to expect can be overwhelming. Though—she is standing taller than I during this time. In hindsight, probably because of her inner strength and the one thing that is scaring me the most—her dementia. Ironic, isn't it?

Yes indeed, upon studying symptoms of dementia, it is said that the person will stay focused on one main subject at a time... which is funny, as we all could benefit from focusing on one thing at a time. Rather, we plan for a future that is truly unknown in most cases of life. Preparation is always a plus, but planning will prove God's sense of humor—always.

So—denial is a moot point currently. Onward and upward... and nerves to no end. Anger shows its ugly face. "I never expected this to happen to Moma." This is so unfair. All the cliché things that one can think of visited my mind. Frustration became common place. Along with the need to learn more about her condition, I was just plumb mad that she had to be going through this... this new "thing" that was part of her now. Part of her.

There—I said it and life still goes on. So, it wasn't the end of the world. Just the beginning of a new phase of our lives... new and unknown.

Grief crept in. Looking back, I can say that it was a combination of fear still hanging on and the loss of our "norm."

Things are changing faster than my mind can keep up. Probably because my mind is still spinning. To add to this drama, let me say that it dawned on my "overactive" mind that now at age 54, I, too, could possibly receive this fate in the far future. The rush is on for medications or meditations, I don't care which, to help Moma and keep my possible fate at bay. Fear, oh yes, I added this extra stress to our already challenging lives. Way to go.

While visiting a friend who lost her mother with Alzheimer's, I found a connection to her and reached out for some guidance. She shared with me a book that started my path to healing. *The 36-Hour Day* by Mace and Rabins gave me direction and an insight that I needed so badly on this new venture. New venture... even my interpretation of this phase of our new lives is softer and more accepting. Might I even say challenging, yet cherished? Vulnerable times are challenging yet can be cherished times. And the "corner has been turned." Been holding my breath with anxiety.

Exhale.

Going through my books, I come across a small piece of paper with Moma's writing and two small smiley stickers—one blue, one green. Moma's and my favorite colors.

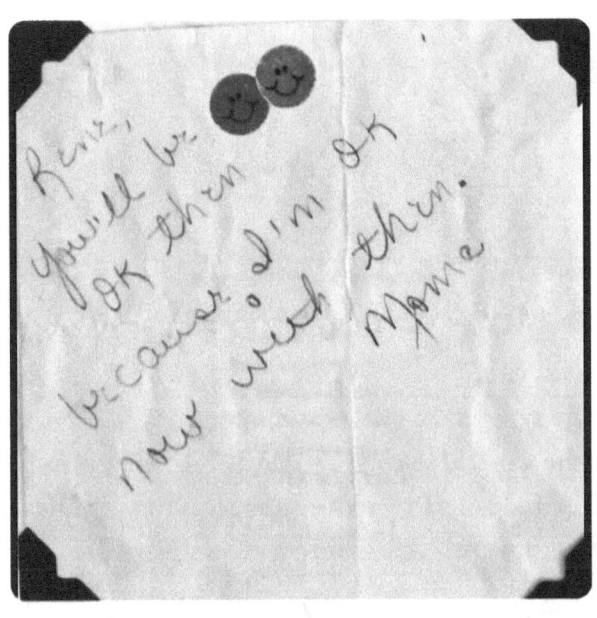

Rene
You'll be OK then because I'm OK now with then.
Moma

Powerful words from an unknown time in our past, yet so meaningful now. I feel Moma's arms around me... holding me saying that all will be well. All is well. Feels so good. I think I'm ready for the next stage that Moma arrived at long before me. I look up and see my husband there waiting for me.

Acceptance.

No Mistakes

Living life now takes on a new dimension. Dimension. Funny that the word is so close to dementia. Thinking about it, dementia does indeed add a new dimension to our lives. Only now we are accepting every day and every change with love as if it were expected. Another "friend," if you will, as we invite a new stage or change into our daily lives. Life has become easier. More relaxed.

Not to say that our new life has no challenges. Oh no, not to say that...

The year is 2010. Moma is new to dementia but finding driving to be more trouble than it's worth. Not so much in her own driving but that of others that find hers annoying... the drivers that have no patience for those of us who find we are in the wrong lane or have made a wrong turn or just want to change our minds while driving.

Then there is Betsy, a 1989 Mercury Grand Marquis. My mom and dad's pride and joy. It, too, wanted to slow down, and Moma found herself visiting the shop for Betsy over and over again. One day while on the way to the shop, a car full of young men looking for "something to do" found harassing my mom to be their entertainment. At a stoplight, they lowered their windows, took off their shoes and started beating on mom's car windows. I get angry just writing this but feel it's important to keep it real. When the light turned green, they sped off, the cowards that they are. Moma pulled over to the side of a four-lane highway and into a parking lot of a little side-street diner. As she got out of her car, a trucker from inside the diner saw her in distress and approached her. Her car had begun smoking again, one of its many times and the reason for her appointment at the shop that day.

Spotting a car sales lot across the highway, Moma decided she wanted to go there. The trucker helped her (all 5 foot 2 and 98 pounds of her) into his rig with a lift. "Just give me a good push on my butt and I will reach the handle." That's my Moma! Upon arriving at the lot, she approached a man who appeared to work there, and asked if he had authority. Turns out he was the owner. "If you take me home, that car across the highway is yours. I choose not to have a car any longer." Wait, what?

Drying my tears, in hindsight, it was probably a blessing to release Betsy at that time … which would really peeve those boys if they thought something good came from their actions. "There are no mistakes," my Moma would say.

Betsy

Now, it's not every day that someone walks into your place and says, "Take my car please." The car lot did everything properly, starting with making sure she was safe. Moma's trucker finally left her, knowing they were taking care of her. They calmed her down and asked oodles of questions. They called me to confirm, which I did, after collecting my emotions.

Then a woman took her home, where she continued her questions, making sure that she understood what she was asking for. Of course, she did—and finally said to the young girl, "I know what you're doing. Checking if I'm all here. I am and I just don't want the stress of my car anymore." That was the end of that!

Betsy ended up going to the owner's daughter, who was about to head off to college. She had an overhaul and is living well to this day. I've saved the plate of Betsy and thank her every day for her part in keeping Moma safe.

Amen.

The Dance

Of course, what is life without a few snags? We encountered the need for transportation to various places like doctor appointments or the bank. We tried the medical ride from Moma's insurance but found it unreliable. Let me say that she refuses to rely on friends or neighbors, and I fear a cab, for I would worry about her safety.

After research, I found Palm Tran Connection which, even with its faults, has been a godsend. Rules needed to be learned—must call by 5 PM the day before your trip, there is a 30-minute window for pickup and return time (which is seldom on time), the fee of $3.00 exact change is required each way, etc. It all works out somehow.

We did experience an issue of her feeling guilty. Unwarranted, but real to her. I found her in tears often when I would make reservations for her. It made me so sad. She explained that it was her need to still feel independent, but making her own reservations was becoming increasingly difficult. There was guilt that, "I had to help her." It took me a while, but I hope I made her see allowing me to help was the greatest gift she could give me.

Our "dance" shifted from time to time with the rhythm going from happy to sad based on the emotions felt by her at that time. Natural feelings—but like anything new, scary. The important thing is to keep dancing—you'll get past any toe stepping and in time, the dance becomes a beautiful waltz.

Hello, Walmart

I was worried with Moma not having a car, it might lead her to becoming closed in and frail. Not. Instead she finds her way to her local Walmart on the corner almost daily. Round trip takes about an hour with walking and time spent shopping. Everyone knows her and her pushcart (her car) that she has made from a roller bag and a luggage pulley. She makes every day a new adventure, "forgetting" her list most all the time. I'm beginning to believe it is on purpose in order to have yet another reason to go tomorrow. A good thing.

Of course, imagine if you will, a little cracked sidewalk shared by walkers, bikes, and pulleys. That alone is therapy, as it requires all your senses to navigate your trip. Once inside Walmart, I can only imagine the derby that begins with the narrow aisles. She gives her "car" a free ride in the carriage and at checkout, she has taught all to pack it properly for her walk home. She rewards them by buying them candy bars. Of course, she saves one for herself. That and lots of potato sticks.

Her pharmacy is there also. Good people, friends I can even call them, though I've never met them. They watch over Moma and take my calls anytime with questions. They even called me to make sure Moma got home one evening, as it was getting dark. Gege, (Gerardine Mendez), my go-to person there, will always jump from behind the counter when she can and visit with Moma, helping her look for anything she needs. She sends me selfies of the two of them. Priceless. Did I say good people? Wonderful people.

Thank you, Gege, for being one of Moma's angels on Earth. You are a godsend.

Nayla

This chapter is dedicated to a little cat named Nayla. To set the stage for this saga, Moma and several of her neighbors got themselves in trouble many times feeding feral cats in their neighborhood. The association went crazy. Oh well. Meanwhile, one of Moma's regulars came in one day for her feeding and decided to give birth in her pantry. What a wonderful experience. Who knew the important role this little angel would play in our lives!

As the babies grew, Moma took them to be adopted and, one by one, they were chosen. All but Nayla. It was God's work in action. So began our lives with Nayla.

This little furball has become Moma's caregiver. Animals have been shown to help us with our moods. They give our day a clock, a routine while caring for them. Fact is, while Moma is caring for Nayla, Nayla is in turn caring for Moma. Nayla's sixth sense seems to know everything from her feelings of happiness to when she needs extra care. She even seems to know when Moma needs to go to the bathroom at night, as she will wake and follow her into the bathroom, stay with her, and escort her back to bed.

At night, when Moma and Nayla go to bed, that little angel waits for her to get settled and close her eyes. She then gives a kiss to each eyelid and settles somewhere on the bed, making sure to be touching her always. I thank God for Nayla every day, as she is to me my mom's keeper. I don't feel as though my mom lives alone—she lives with Nayla.

Routine

"I threw out my TV."

"What? Moma, what do you mean?"

"I threw it downstairs because I don't enjoy watching it anymore."

Well, I have learned that with dementia, your interest span is short and in hindsight—it was a very old TV, with an old picture and sound to match. Of course, I got nervous when she said to me that she never watched it anyway, as she watches the 6:30 evening news every day. Ritual. Something to do. Call it anything you want, but how to get the TV back? I asked her to please bring it back into her home. She fought me a lot, as I was overriding what she wanted and felt was best. It was a bit of a struggle, but I promised her that she needn't plug it in if she didn't want to.

As it turned out, she did try plugging it in, only to say the scratches from rolling it down her stairs made the picture worse. OK, please have your neighbor take it back downstairs this time—and no more talk of TV, I promised her.

A few days went by and I feared the change in ritual. We thought of a radio. Palm Tran Connection time, off to the store, and Moma now has music in her kitchen. Life is good.

A few days passed. One day Moma shared with me that she had a gecko and her two babies in her house. Not absurd, as she does live in South Florida, where these little critters are plentiful.

She said they kept popping their heads out from behind the picture hanging in her kitchen. No telling how long they had lived there. She kept trying to sweep them out to the front porch, but they would end up behind the picture in the kitchen again. Now I knew. Moma was having delusions.

Later that night, with the lighting low and the lack of routine from TV, Moma found herself upset about a bug on the floor. She called over her neighbor to have her check it out. It turned out to be one of Nayla's cat toys. Then Nayla's teddy bear, leaning on the ladder, began to move. Her neighbor explained that it was the fur of the bear moving due to her ceiling fan being on.

Yet later—on the phone with Moma, she explained how the bear was just "showing off now, dancing on one leg, holding the ladder." She asked me if she was losing it. I assured her that this was perfectly normal with the late hour of the day, low lighting, and the change of routine. She kept asking me what she should do about the bear. I said "Moma, that bear is there for your entertainment. If you want to watch him—do so. If you don't want to watch him, then just look away." We both laughed and another "stepping-stone" was placed, with us holding each other, balancing well.

Even the teddy bear.

Thoughts

"When I get to Heaven, they don't have long-distance phone service. What are we going to do?"

I promised Moma that they will, and that we will, ALWAYS be "next door, next door." I have learned these thoughts that pop out are very normal and common. In the beginning I made more out of them than needed. "Where did that come from?" What should I say? Truth is...treat them as "normal" as they are. We have always had thoughts that come to mind, only now they fall out of the mouth as well. Happens to all of us to various degrees.

When I turned 50, I gained more confidence to speak my mind without care. Now, soon to be 55...look out :-) Dementia will sometimes cause "mouth to overload butt," as my daddy would say. Own it. Deal with it. Move on.

Granny's Ways

Granny would tell her girls to take their ailments to the tree in their backyard. Making a small cut in the bark would cause the tree to seep. They would then place the sap on their wounds or pain, "taking it to nature for healing." She also had a wonderful way of helping her six girls with life. In their early years, Granny would give them paper and pencil. Some, not of age to write, would draw their problems on paper. Spending time on detail, knowing that Granny would want to see these drawings, this action would usually cause the issue to resolve itself or become less grand. By placing it on paper, it didn't seem as large. Drawings contained on a piece of paper seem smaller, more manageable.

As they grew older, they were able to write things down... a ritual that Moma and I do to this day. Likewise, words on paper seem less daunting, and seeing the words helps us find our way through them.

Ironic, since Granny couldn't read or write, but somehow knew that by placing your thoughts, drawn or written, on paper, it would give you time to think on it and usually help find an answer.

I can say that the age of computers to monitor her medications and pay her bills online is a godsend. I still keep things in order with Granny's list concept. Modern medicine is wonderful, but you can't dismiss the simple beauty of yesteryear to keep life ready for tomorrow. Thank you, Granny.

Simple Things

"I walked to Walmart, had a wonderful time, got back home and found my teeth."

Oh well. Teeth are optional, after all. I mean, until you want to eat. Your hat to block the hot summer sun is a must, cash would be a plus... underwear, please. Once Moma leaned over in her hallway (thank goodness) and felt a cold bum as she mooned the wall.

We all experience "funnies." I love sharing Moma's with her. I mean, what is life without funnies?

Stressful—boring.

If more people would look for the funnies in their day, there would be more smiles in the world.

Then there are the times of trash picking. In Moma's association, people who are moving will leave their belongings downstairs by the trash canisters. It becomes a "yard sale" for all to enjoy. Furniture is one item that shows up a lot... and small beauties like vases or odd dishes. "Goodies," if you will. It's not a matter of needing these items... just finding them is fun! Again, the little things in life.

Funnies and goodies. Life should be that simple.

Chocolate

Some days you just need chocolate. Seems this is the only thing that does the trick. These are the days that nothing really bad is happening—but things just aren't coming together. Today was one of those days.

Moma's doctor visit went well, thank God. She enjoyed Walmart. Her doctor's office even called me back the same day! Of course, the entire message was that her visit went well, her circulation was good, and her next appointment is April 12 at 8:30 AM. Okay—but what's missing is the core of the visit. Questions that seem to be missed. Why is Moma having red swelling in her legs and throbbing with the feeling of "rain" down them? What can be done to ease her discomfort?

All that said, I'm still very grateful for her doctor, as at least I have the peace of mind that "all is well" with Moma—which is the first and foremost issue. While brainstorming with John, he suggested she take a Tylenol for her pain. It helped. I guess God made us to pick up where the doctors leave off. Snickers candy bar, please.

Part 2
Keeping It Real

March 2013 – May 2013

Moma in 1944, age 14 (on the right), with her sister Bertha Mae.

Life Keeps Going

Keeping it real... I find dementia can cause fear from loss of control. I find routine things are now becoming complicated; confusion can set in. Wait—am I speaking of Moma's or my own life?

Truly, we have only control of our own actions and then some control of our life events. Any one of us, with dementia or not, will find that life is full of surprises. The feeling of fear can visit us all. It's an ugly but natural part of life. Our normal instinct is to protect our loved ones by finding a way to make it all better. "All better." What does that mean? How does it work? Okay... back to keeping it real.

"Don't chew more than you can swallow." Wise words from Moma... her version of "Don't bite off more than you can chew." Works for me :-)

Sometimes life keeps going while you're trying to figure out what to do next. Slow down. Cry. Breathe. Smile. It's all good,

Atwaba, Sussy*

---

* *Atwaba was created from my childhood of saying to Moma, "I love you all the world and back again." "Sussy" is the name of a stuffed bear we bought in Colombia, which speaks Spanish. She says several things, one of which is her name. I played it often for Moma to bring back her memories.*

Viewpoints

"I think I'll start heading down to Walmart now—it's 11:25 in the morning."

"Actually, Moma, it's 8:10 in the morning. Your clock's off."

"No, no, I'm just reading it sideways."

Funny, but if you take the time to lean back in your chair and glance at the clock sideways, she was reading the same "time" as me, only seeing something different. So appropriate when you think about it as it represents life as a whole. Two completely different conclusions from the same point. Each correct in their own viewpoint.

Of course, in this case, Moma soon realized that she needed to wait a little bit for the store to open. But the simplicity of her answer for the incorrect time was classic. Nothing huge. Nothing to be embarrassed about, as in reality, her view of the clock made sense. "Sideways" aside, she saw her own correct time.

If we could always take a pause to realize that a different conclusion may not be a "wrong" conclusion, but rather one's own interpretation of the viewpoint, life becomes easier.

Moma's Birthday

Happy birthday to you. Happy birthday to you.
Happy birthday, dear Moma. Happy birthday to YOU.

boop-boop March 10, 2013
We'll do this again next year!

Atwaba—Sussy

Dear Moma,
You came into this world and made it a better place by just being here. The lives you have touched, the difference you make in all you do and all you share is such a blessing. I am so very grateful that you were born and that I was born to YOU. I love you "all the world and back again"!

—"Little" Rene

Just Life

"I'm heading out to Walmart. If I don't answer my cell phone...I forgot it at home."

So often we think the worst when things don't go as planned. When I call Moma on her cell or at home, and she doesn't answer, my nerves set in. In "my own little script of this day" Moma answers her phone when it rings, and all is well. Nowhere in the script did I see she was napping or cleaning out the closet or walking down to Walmart with her phone on the kitchen table. Let's get real: we might like to think we write the script, but we, in no way, direct it!

The sooner we realize this bit of information, the better off we are. Of course, for some dumb reason, we still try to be the "director of our day"—planning our schedule and writing down lists of things to do. One should have an idea of what their day may hold. Only we might want to see the broader picture of life and not be overwhelmed by it.

"If I don't answer the phone, I forgot it." That simple. Nothing wrong. No drama. Just life.

Thank you, Moma.

Changes

Another pretty day out. Funny how the day affects our moods. Understandable really, even scientifically proven. No surprise here. Yet if you think about it, your "world" is made up of so much more than what's outside your window. Sure, we have the need to go out in that icky day for work or appointments… or even to walk our dog. But our lives are so much more.

Moma finds her life comfortable in her home with Nayla. A sense of privacy and independence, her "own space," if you will. Not to say that she mightn't get restless. She has been known to clean the same pantry or drawer time and again. "Rearranging," she says. Even moving furniture around—if Nayla approves of it, of course. This gives her a sense of accomplishment. Not to mention the physical and mental exercise she gets out of it.

Now let's get back to the pretty day out and not forget to thank God for the marketplace on her corner. When we first moved into our home some 27 years ago, it was a very woodsy area. Part of its charm, even. Through the years, we watched it change. More buildings, wider roads, shops on every corner. Moma's corner. Funny how life turns out. How things seem to come together when our need is there. What drew us to this place years ago—though very changed today, is better than ever for Moma—now. God's plan.

Life's Lists

"We all have a place where we put our important "notes to self." Mine is on my coffee table, aka my desk.

Moma uses her lamp in her kitchen. Lamp*shade*, actually. I envision a fast-food diner with the slips of paper attached to the wheel in a pass-through service window. They spin it around, pull down another order, and before you know it, they ring that bell and your food is ready. Voila.

This came to be, partially thanks to Nayla. Where I leave mine on a table, I do find things on the floor, thanks to our dogs from time to time. Add a cat to the equation, and Nayla finds "good fun" in watching papers fly off the table. Now envision Moma's lampshade filled with clothes pins and notes of all sizes. Pretty clever idea, if you ask me. Seems to work well, with the exception of her grocery list. Moma heads off to Walmart every time leaving her list at home. Like I've said before, subliminally, I think it is to have yet another reason to go back tomorrow.

Life is busy, sometimes hard to keep up with. Keep makings lists.

Keep trying…

Shake It Off

So, there are "those days" when sadness kicks in. Sadness for the distance of my mom. Sadness of her dementia. Sadness in general. Today was one of those days. Sitting "sadly" on the sofa, I tried to pinpoint the issue. No one individual issue. Just stuff. I stated to John that I wished Moma lived closer. He agreed...but then quietly reminded me that all but the distance would be the same if Moma were next door. Dementia is not different whether in Florida or Massachusetts...actually for Moma, the change of environment would be very difficult. So, he discussed that having Moma here would be better for me, but not for Moma, until she is ready.

This put a reality check on my sadness. "My sadness." Made me think outside myself and realize that Moma was having a better day than I was. I smiled, laughed even, at the broad picture of how we can so easily get sucked into our own "pity party." Shaking it off and seeing issues in a more positive light, I feel pretty lucky, even blessed with ALL aspects of our lives and am ready to embrace what life brings us next.

Small Is Small

One day Moma and I were sharing our issues of getting older. I have no issue with my gray hairs, as I think it adds distinction. I'm chunky enough that my face has very few wrinkles for my age. My neck is my thing! I joke that when I shake my head, my neck waves in agreement! Ugh.

This, along with perimenopause, mood swings, hot flashes, weight gain, arthritis, bursitis, "woe-itis." The fun is endless…

Moma was sharing with me that when in her store surrounded with seniors, breaking gas is inevitable. Just keeping it real. Of course, no one knows who the culprit is and of course, everyone points fingers :-)

The other day Moma said something that I think is priceless…

"We might be 'losing it,' but we're not taking responsibility for God's doing. God gives us gas, we let it pass. That simple."

Remember the small things in life are, well, small.

Trust

"You need to have faith in God and trust your guardian angel."
Strong words to live by. Hard to do sometimes, as when things get tough, we have the reaction to grab onto something solid. Out comes our instinct to start a plan of "fixing it." Figure it out. Write it down. Plan and proceed. Brainstorm.

Fail is not one of the words in your plan. Yet failure is human. Sometimes, you just can't fix it—but you can still make it right. By slowing down and backing off from the issue. By getting a clearer understanding of what is and isn't in your control. By fighting the fight, you can win … and knowing which fights are out of your reach and how to accept "those" fights.

Truth is that some things are just not in our control. Not today. Maybe tomorrow, but not now. And for these times, our human instinct wants to be childlike and cause a fuss. If you must—do so, and then remember Moma's words…

"You need to have faith in God and trust your guardian angel." Thank you, Moma :-)

Part 3
Rainy Days and Periwinkles

May 2013 – July 2013

Moma in 1947, age 17.

A Day in May

"I think I may be losing my memory…"

Classic words from Moma today, May 6, 2013. We both chuckled and moved on.

Enough said.

Quintessential

Quite some time has passed since I last put thoughts to paper. Not due to lack of interesting moments, but rather that life has been very full of late. Full of both happy and sad times. "Quintessential life." Rainy days that make Moma sad, since she can't walk to Walmart. Happiness when she finds periwinkles along her walk.

On my end, injury at my job, now in recovery, has allowed me time at home to reconnect with my painting—pure joy. Funny how, if you look very closely, for every sadness you can find some joy that will arise from it. Maybe not right away, but don't stop looking. Life is full of looking. We look for comfort. We look for reason. Always look for love and friendship. And as Moma says, "Happiness, health, and peace of mind."

"Quintessential words." Never stop looking…

Circles and Swirls

As a child growing up overseas, some might think that I missed out on so much. How wrong they would be. By living in different cultures and countries, it helped to make me the person I am today.

Coloring books were very hard to come by, if at all. Moma came up with the idea of a plain piece of paper and a pencil. With these two items alone, I would draw randomly, in circles and swirls, to create my own, one-of-a-kind drawing. Out would come the crayons, as many as could be found, both long and short stubs were equally important, as one was as rare as the other. The idea was to color each space with a different crayon to create a beautiful collage of design and color. Choosing the right colors was always important.

Some colors naturally seem to go well together. Others offset each other, while still others stand alone, popping off the page. I remember a crayon called Carnation Pink that would "pop." Of course, it always looked better if you chose a color beside it that complemented it. This lesson learned at an early age taught me so much. For starters, learn to make do with what you have and find some unique joy in the gift. Make your "circles and swirls" in life as pretty as you can, understanding that the choices you make will be yours to color. Lastly, choose your crayons well, as these are what bring your "picture" to life. There will always be an element of grayer, softer colors in life, but remember to pick up those "carnation pinks" and color wildly.

Ironic. I am an artist today, creating originals. I started many years ago... thank you, Moma.

Moma with her favorite Gardening Angel mug.

Peaks and Valleys

"Many yesterday's ago,"—this is how Moma started her sentence with me the other day. Not "long ago" or "many years ago," but "many yesterday's ago." I like it. It gives each day significance, individually. Allows you to look back on your life and see stages, pictures of events. All important in their own time, yet combined, helping to make you the person you are today and helping to prepare you for your tomorrows.

If we can remember to face our tomorrows one day at a time, they don't seem as daunting when issues arise. I believe it is best that we can't see our future. Plan for it, yes. Dream of it, always. But live it day to day to enjoy, or recover, from issues as they come. Treat each day anew. This allows us to make changes we may need as we go. Trust me, changes will become part of who you are. For our lives are filled with new surprises, unexpected challenges, and warm joys. If we can learn to embrace change, our days can become a flow of peaks and valleys allowing us the time to find our way. May you always find yours.

:-)

How Lucky Are We?

"The only distance between us is the mileage."
A heartwarming sentiment from Moma today. How lucky are we?!

The Path Beyond

I asked my husband today where my earphones were. He responded—"I know I put them somewhere."
Really?
That was a great directive. Remember that life gets busy for us all. Our brains get overly full of "stuff" causing the routine things to sometimes become complicated, even without dementia.

I can only imagine how complicated life becomes with dementia. I have noticed of late that Moma and I will be carrying on a vibrant conversation, only to hear a pause followed by "So, what are we talking about?" We have learned to laugh at these moments as they make us realize that maybe whatever it was must not be that important after all... in the scope of things.

I find it helps if I take myself away from the moment and view the larger picture. That one "snag" before you—may seem grand, but if you zoom out, you can see the road that follows it. Instead of seeing the obstacle, you see the path beyond.

I've learned this method even more now with Moma. At first, each issue that would arise, I tried to address with full force. Subliminally, I believe I thought that I could tackle each issue and help control somehow the dementia itself.

After slamming into a brick wall headfirst, I still tried to manage as much as possible. I prepared myself with any information regarding Moma that I could gather. This has been a godsend when helping with medical or household issues that arise. This step should never be skipped.

Which brings us to now. Where we are now will help keep both Moma and me calm. With the "zooming out" from the situation stage, it helps to make the issue smaller. Though still very real, it keeps your eye on the path and journey beyond.

Always enjoy the journey.

Caregiver

Moma said something to me today that made me smile all the way down "to the bottom of my feet." She thanked me for being her caregiver.

It's been four years since Moma was diagnosed with the onset of dementia. Every day she thanks me for all I do, but today was different. Today she went to the bank and then bought a pair of capri pants at Walmart. She traveled on the Palm Tran Connection, which I booked yesterday. Bus was a little late this morning for pickup. I called to learn its whereabouts and made sure that Moma knew. I enjoy calling her from beginning to end, as if I were there with her on her trip. Once home, I feel so happy that she has had a good day. She then gets comfy and settles in for the night with Nayla.

"Caregiver."

Of all the roles I play—daughter, wife, mom, friend, employee, neighbor...being Moma's caregiver has taught me more about life and myself than any.

It's funny Moma thanked me for being her caregiver. I thank her for allowing it and making me a better person.

Story of Life

I share with Moma every chapter I write. We enjoy the laughs and endure the tears. We relive the past and talk about the moment. Sometimes Moma will add her thoughts and memories. Other times she listens and takes it all in. Funny, when I was a child, she would read me stories at night. Now we share our story of life, together.

"Smooth as peanut butter."

Part 4
Living Life

August 2013 – October 2013

Moma in 1948, age 18, with Dad (Robert Terry), age 29, in Daytona Beach, Florida.

Enjoy Simple Pleasures

I have a saying that "life gets in the way of living." By the time I get through all of life's little issues, be it dishes and laundry or walking dogs and cleaning bird cages, my "living" seems to be complete for yet another day. Sometimes I feel overwhelmed with my days, as I'm sure we all do. But then I hear about Moma's simple pleasures of walking to Walmart or the art of rearranging the furnishings in her home, only to put everything back as per Nayla. Makes me smile. That is living at its best!

I was speaking to a friend today and found myself saying "It's always something…" to which she replied, "As it's supposed to be." Gave me a reality check.

It's all good.

Life's Puzzles

Moma was talking about life today and instead of saying her life presents problems, she said that life is full of "puzzles." I like it a lot. Think about it. If we perceived our problems in life as puzzles to be solved, it changes the whole view of that "problem." Now it's not so grand, facing us down, but rather a puzzle that comes in pieces to be re-created into a complete picture.

No longer an issue to be reckoned with, it is now something to work on—to make complete and turn into an asset rather than a pile of pieces. Brings a feeling of accomplishment, achievement. Moves us forward.

Beautiful.

Supposed to Be

Moma thanked me today for "putting up" with her. I responded with the same back to her—but for me! Of course, she was speaking of her forgetfulness getting in her way from time to time. She said that it's only going to get worse. To which I replied, "As it's supposed to be."

As it's supposed to be.

Truth be told, I have those times that I get sad or miss the way things used to be. I still feel frustration for this detour in our lives, and fear might creep in from time to time. But all in all, things are going along just as they are "supposed to." Life flows along... sometimes at a trickle pace and other times more of a splash! Our story is really no different from others being lived next door or halfway around the world. We might feel our story is unique but really, we are all busy living similar lives... with problems, illness, failures... joys, triumphs, and miracles.

Enjoy.

Circle of Prayer

Moma was on her way home from one of her many trips to Walmart. Having turned the corner and on the home stretch to her door, her cart full of groceries became harder for her to pull. Out of nowhere came a man that was, as it turned out, working on a moving truck of a neighbor's home. English was not his language. Still, he spoke to Moma and waited. She, in turn, motioned "all is well" and that she was heading home. This "conversation" went back and forth a bit, followed by the man lifting and carrying her heavy cart to and up her stairs...leaving it at her door with a smile.

This, alone, is a beautiful story, as someone reached out to help my mom. But there's more. While Moma motioned for him to wait, as she intended to tip him, he was gone upon her return. An act of kindness with nothing expected in return. A novel thought in this day and age. Makes me smile. Also makes me realize that there really is "something in return."

How so, you ask?

Being so far away in distance from Moma, I pray for her safety and the kindness of others toward her daily. For this prayer, I will do my best to give kindness to all that cross my path. My prayers are answered and returned.

If more people could find this path, there would be so much more kindness in the world and giving to each other.

Think about that.

Good Talk

I have begun to notice that less is more. When it comes to explaining something to Moma, the less words used, the better understood. On the times that stories are repeated, laugh and listen as if for the first time. When asked why you didn't share something before now, knowing that you did, merely say "I might have... but" and move on. All of these newly learned tricks are an asset these days. Before dementia, Moma and I would talk endlessly, weaving in and out of issues and subjects... never missing a beat. We still talk endlessly, only now weaving in and out of subjects is more of a trait than a trend. I love when Moma gets off the subject—goes down an alternate conversation path in depth, pauses and says "So, what's that got to do with anything?" Love that!

I always say, "I'm not sure, but it was a great story!" We both laugh and feel good. That's what matters.

Dementia changes your life.

"Simply stated, it's that complicated."

You must change along with it, then all will be well :-)

Part 5
Be Still

October 2013 – November 2013

Moma in 1950, age 20, with Dad, age 31, at Pier Casino, Daytona Beach, Florida.

Be Still and Know

"One day at a time." An old cliché and still a wonderful mantra today. Life gets busy. It can get complicated. If you spend your time like me, overthinking everything, you can become crazy.

"Be still and know I am God."

Psalm 46:10. So few words—such strong meaning. Live it, and life is easier. A problem shared is half when held. I have been trying to share my problems with God and then the weight of my issues is less.

Be still.

Moma's Round Table

This chapter is dedicated to Moma's round table. The kitchen table is the center of her home and activities.

It has her daily agenda, her lamp with her important papers pinned to the shade, cards when playing solitaire, and potato sticks when snacking. Nayla loves to sprawl across it for back rubs. Many a conversation has been shared with Moma while sitting at her table.

We've had many laughs, shared some tears, and solve the "problems of the world." Needless to say, it is the heartbeat of her home.

Did you notice I called it the *round table*? That's because it is... round. Round in a square world, allowing things to find their way to the edge and off to the floor on several, might I say *many*, occasions. Consider it entertainment, or maybe daily exercise, that Moma is faced with this challenge. Constantly rearranging... always picking up off the floor. Why doesn't she change the table out for a square one, you ask? Well...

For starters, that would mean exchanging one issue with that of another. Square isn't all that great. You can bang the heck out of yourself on those corners. That could be longer lasting than picking stuff up. Then there is the sentiment, the personal feeling one gets over the long period of time spent with someone or something. It feels like it belongs there. Part of you.

In hindsight... one could say it is better to work with a little issue than to trade for a larger problem :-)

Treasures from Home

When Moma was driving, she would go to the thrift shops almost daily for the thrill of finding the one item that we had no idea we were in need of. Small things that we weren't sure what they were. Large things that were very useful. Lots of books and tapes. Always a squeaky toy for each dog, along with doggy treats. Over time, we ended up with LOTS of clocks for John. We could've opened a store. Silk flowers for my garden, gadgets for the unknown, teddy bears for my collection (one of many). Clothes, lots of clothes for wearing out, house clothes, some for gardening and others for sleeping. Sometimes there were food items I couldn't find up North. Boiled peanuts and barbecued pork, along with chocolate malted milk…mmm.

All that said, it was great fun receiving our boxes from Moma. We had it down pat: media mail for books and tapes, regular mail for all other treasures. Every box was a happy dance in the making, until trying to find room for these treasures in our little apartment. We started receiving boxes once a month. Then, losing track, it became every other week. On some occasions, there were two at a time, as it was easier to send two small ones rather than one large one. Short of the drama of space, all boxes were a touch of Moma and were always pure joy!

Last Box

Life gets busy and time is never enough. Our apartment got flooded due to a washing machine pipe bursting. We were packed out of our home for seven weeks while all was repaired. Packed out, along with all our belongings, was one of Moma's book boxes. This box became the "last one" of our box story. I found myself moving it from place to place unopened. First, it was due to lack of furniture, as we lost quite a bit and took time to replace everything. But soon I realized the true meaning of why I wasn't opening it.

Since the mailing of this one box, as you have read thus far, life had changed. Life always does. We are the lucky ones—who can find joy within those changes and embrace them. I can say that we have and are doing just that. If you look for it, there is joy somewhere in every day.

Now back to the box, the last box. The end of an era. A small part of me felt that if I didn't open it, somehow, I was holding on to the way things were and magically Moma wouldn't get worse. To the logical mind, I realized this was baloney. But to the deeper, inner childlike mind, I just couldn't bring myself to open it. Until today.

Three years almost to the day from the posted date, I opened "the box." First, I smiled and touched each thing as if I were touching Moma, knowing she was the last to touch these gifts.

Then I had my own personal cry for the closure of a period that we shared and enjoyed so much. Afterwards, calling Moma was like old times. We visited each item, reliving the time she spent at her Goodwill store. There was no sadness thought of, but instead, pure joy coming from this little box of books and tapes.

I put the last book on my bookshelf and smiled. A flood of emotions hit me again… memories, laughter, clutter, joy, tears, reality of today's new chapter still in progress.

I kept the empty box :-)

Part 6
Making Every Day Count

January 2014 – March 2014

Moma in 1953, age 23.

Lead or Follow—Just Keep Going

I must say that in the scope of things, Moma's dementia is progressing slowly, thank God. It's been over four years now. We've had lots of uphill climbing, speed bumps popping up when least expected, tears, fears—and laughter! What else can you do, when you think about it? You know what's happening, you have an idea of what's coming. Yet you want to find joy in every day, something to be happy about.

Truth be told, you don't truly know what is ever going to happen. Everyone experiences some common traits, but there are such variables that make your own dementia uniquely yours. Then there are the ever-changing symptoms … some days are clearer than others, like the sky itself. Only, you can't tell by the cloud coverage what type of day you might be in for. Always bring an umbrella :-)

But isn't that "life" after all? We only *think* we have a grip on things. Life happens to everyone. It only matters how we choose to dance to it. Sometimes you lead. Other times, life itself is leading you. All we can do is feel the moment and dance as fast as we can.

Making a Difference

Several weeks back, Moma was walking to Walmart and noticed a wild bush overtaken by a weed. With TLC, she took her time and untangled the weed to free the chocking bush. A simple act, really. One that takes little time and merely the effort to notice.

In life, these two things are used less than should be. More and more, people find themselves with less. Less time in our lives, less time to find the small wonders of joy. Less time to make a difference.

Time passed, and Moma shared with me today that her rescued bush is thriving and beautiful. She is so happy to have made that difference. Made me smile and realize that we can all learn from this "simple act" that gives of ourselves yet gives much more in return.

Jeans

Moma threw out an old pair of jeans that were frayed on the bottom but still comfy. Afterwards, she thought better of it and realized they could be useful for house pants or gardening. Of course, they were in the trash canister downstairs. This posed no problem for Moma :-)

Down the stairs, carrying her ladder, she went. She placed the ladder beside the trash canister and climbed in. While rummaging for the bag with her jeans, she heard a man's voice saying, "This ladder is perfect," as he grabbed it and started to walk away. She called out to him, with no response. Now standing up in the canister, she shouted out to him that she was using that ladder. His response was not shock that she was standing in the trash can but rather, "I didn't know where that voice was coming from." All said and done, Moma got her jeans back, climbed out of the canister with his help and yes, kept the ladder for next time.

Makes me realize that even when we feel something is old and useless, on second thought, it can become a prized possession. She washed and wore them that night... and smiled.

Retirement

Moma was talking today about the blessing of living in Florida, where she can walk all year long and keep healthy. We laugh when I share with her the weather for her day, only to have her ask about ours. Hers being in the 70s, while ours has been in the teens and single digits of late, not counting the wind chill. The funniest thing she said was she didn't want to think about moving up this way... at least until she retires.

Retires?

I love it! Makes me realize that she views her life as being vibrant and happy, with only her and Nayla to attend to. They have their routines and the comfort of their home. They find joy in every day.

What else is there?

One on One

Moma and I were talking tonight about life. Her life with Nayla. Mine with John and our three dogs and five birds. And of course, Moma's and my life shared every day. She occasionally feels bad for Nayla being an only animal vs. our petting zoo. I reminded her that, though our entourage of "babies" are very happy sharing life, there is just as much joy found in the solitude of "one on one." Nayla feels that she is Moma's care partner and in truth, she is. She shares every moment of Moma's life—be it the happy dance for no reason in the middle of the afternoon or the sobbing cry due to an overwhelming moment in life. Animals feed off our emotions and respond accordingly. They never question or judge, but merely appreciate sharing our moment with us. I thank God for Nayla being Moma's "one on one" every day.

Moma's Birthday

March 10, 2014

Happy birthday to you. Happy birthday to you.
Happy birthday, dear Moma. Happy birthday to YOU.

boop-boop March 10, 2014.
We'll do this again next year!!

Atwaba—Sussy

Dear Moma,

Our life story in this journal has been in the making for over a year now. I have to say that so much has happened in this time and what a gift it is to live each moment with you. What laughs we've shared! The tears have been few, but important as well… and when shared are dried even faster. I give thanks for each day I share with you. I love you "all the world and back again"!!

—"Little" Rene

Classic Moma. Enjoying a birthday banana split, 1980.

Part 7
Breathe and Feel Blessed

March 2014 – June 2014

Moma in 1956, age 26.

Interpretation

It's amazing that one issue can be viewed so differently. It came to my attention this week that Moma has not been taking all her medications correctly—for some time now. I became instantly overwhelmed and scared. Guilt came over me for failing to know. How did this happen... I covered all bases... didn't I? I'm always asking if her pills are in order, thinking that if I keep addressing it, her memory would be jarred, and this would keep it fresh in her mind. I also have the relationship with her pharmacy at Walmart as my backup. Right?

Yet, during a dementia outburst, Moma said to me that she wished there was a pill to help with anxiety. I gently reminded her there is and asked if she had taken it that day. Boom. Reality check. She has been taking her thyroid pill and fully understands the importance of this. All other medications, all bets are off.

Let me say here that Moma's ailments, overall, required only her thyroid pill daily. Other than that, physically, her health is better than mine. We had been adding other meds because of her dementia. With the realization that my false feeling of security was coming apart, I calmly called her pharmacy. Moma's medications often were filled at her doctor's office during visits, so it was not alarming to them that she hadn't filled a script at her pharmacy. That, along with "no more refills" on the bottle, caused yet another loophole. She interpreted "no more refills" as having completed that script. In her mind, she did just that.

I would have never thought of this being an issue. Makes you see how real one's interpretation can be. I got her in to see her doctor the same week and was told she is doing great.

Do the very best you can and "kiss the rest up to God," as Moma so often says.

Breathe and feel blessed.

Vulnerability

Vulnerability is a real issue when sharing life with someone with dementia. I notice when Moma has a moment of confusion, however small or "normal" it is, fear of my seeing her as "weak" makes the matter much worse. No one wants to feel or appear vulnerable, but if that person has confusion, being vulnerable becomes a liability. I find that Moma not only gets upset with herself but becomes overly "protective" of her confusion so as to not be seen by others. If noticed by me, she feels that the burden of protection will then fall on me. This—rather than seeing it is a privilege for me to do anything possible to make her life better and safe.

There is a fine line between holding on and letting go. I find that if I hold on too tight, it makes her feel childlike and I am seen as the one directing or scolding, even though not intended. Then if I let go too much, I would be horrified if something were to happen to her and I could have prevented such or made it easier for her.

Funny, with all these words ... the best you can do is the best you can—followed by prayer and trust in God.

Moma's Tree

There is a tree in front of Moma's home that has been there from the beginning. She used to plant impatiens around it and watched it grow over the many years.

We were told it is a male olive tree. Both Moma and Daddy used to fuss about the stuff that would fall on their car, as their parking spot was right next to it. Daddy would wash Betsy, the car, endlessly. Still, they loved the tree. People would stop and comment on how beautiful her flowers were around the base. It made her happy.

Time passes and Betsy is off to her new home. Moma no longer plants impatiens around the base, yet the tree still finds a way to be in her life. She enjoys watching the rustling of the leaves. She sees the shadows made by the sunlight shining through into her kitchen. The longevity and stability of the tree over the years has made it an old friend.

The base of the tree now bears its roots. One side is solid to the ground, while the other side, roots are exposed. The tree has small, fingerlike roots that come up and over the larger ones, almost like anchoring to strengthen the base. It's quite incredible to see that nature is so in tune with its own changes in life … being aware when the tree needed a helping hand. No doctors to give guidance. No special medications. Just nature doing what needs to be done. Beautiful.

Makes me think that though we, in life, do benefit from Western ways of doctors and medicine, nothing—but nothing takes the place of nature and the course of time.

Moma looking at her tree (just beyond the lamppost), all grown up.

Sharing Clouds

We see the sky every day, yet very seldom do any of us really look at it. We enjoy the sunshine, complain about the rain, and depending on your age, either enjoy or tolerate the snow. It's all a part of life and for the most part, happens without a thought.

Moma asked me today if we can see the same clouds. "Of course," I said. It made us seem closer that we were, looking at the same clouds—at the same time, sharing, if you will. Of course, we aren't seeing the exact same clouds, but overall, we are viewing the same sky.

Distance is merely a word. Closeness is a state of mind and heart. Moma and I could never be closer than we are right now. So today we will look to the sky and share our day by watching the clouds float by.

Birthday Month

Today I am feeling extra honored to have my relationship with Moma.

Things have changed. June used to be my "birthday month" and every morning's conversation would start with "Happy birthday month" from Moma. Now June fades into the calendar year and my birthday happens to be in there somewhere. Somewhere... we need to remember that our loved one is still "in there somewhere," though scattered and slightly confused, wanting to remain the same.

Moma is still the same person. She begged me to remind her that today is my birthday, as it is still important to her to remain the same. It's hardest on us, the caregivers, to witness these changes in our loved one. I just keep feeling the core of our bond that is ever strong, maybe stronger now than ever before. I keep feeling blessed to have her in any capacity. Her heart sill beats the same. Her mind is different, though if you fasten your seat belt, it can be an adventurous ride.

The weather is good this morning for her walk to Walmart. Teeth in, money in girdle, she's on her way to find periwinkles and smiling.

How blessed are we??

50-50

Fifty percent of me is still viewing Moma's dementia as her baby girl, always wanting—needing her to be doing okay. Any glimmer of hope is built up in my mind as a great day. I "will" it to be... need it to be.

The other 50 percent of me is Moma's caregiver. I look for changes that come. Some subtle, while others come barreling up and I pray to have the knowledge and strength to make it better. Some things we laugh about, some we cry. Others require changes to be made. Change never comes easy.

Moma is still very lucid. She repeats endlessly but will respond to any statement with complete clarity and conviction. Though her reality will be clouded, it still makes complete sense, even to the clear minded. This, along with her dementia, makes her situation 50–50. Fifty percent of her is fragile and in need of guidance to keep her flowing in the best direction. The other 50 percent is still very strong, maybe in denial, but lucid. This makes any guidance very difficult to offer, as her strong side steps in while her fragile side does not see consequences. What a twist of fate. Two parts of me dancing with two parts of Moma as fast as we can.

What else is there to do but dance?

"All is well."

Part 8
Road Trip

July 9, 2014 – July 28, 2014

Moma in 1958, age 28.

Life's Surprise

Funny how we know something is inevitable, yet when faced with the issue, we become clouded and anxious. Seems no matter how much you prepare for something, life can still take you by surprise.

Here in these next few chapters is our story of one sudden "surprise"…

The Drive Begins

Let me start by saying that one week ago, Moma fell off a ladder while trying to change a light bulb. I could say it was her dementia causing her poor judgment, but in truth, it was also her stubbornness, to feel nothing is beyond her grasp. After her fall, Moma's routine changed. Pain stops most people. Her walks to Walmart became too difficult. Repeated days of staying in caused one day to flow into the other. Time had no meaning. Sleep would creep in—on and off during the day, disrupting sound sleep at night.

Wanting Moma to see the doctor, she became overwhelmed at the thought of going into his office. I had her neighbor check her body for any bruises or possible cuts. Thank God, there was no physical damage that could be seen. Emotionally, however, she became lethargic due to lack of exercise and loss of structure in her life. Variance of any norm exacerbates dementia. Crying came easily. Life became harder.

John and I started the drive south to take care of Moma and assess everything.

Florida Orange Juice

We opted to drive rather than fly, due to our own medical issues and not being sure if we might bring Moma back north with us if needed. Fifteen hundred miles equates to two nights on the road and three 8 to 10-hour days of driving. On day three of our drive it was John's 60th birthday. We stopped at the Florida Welcome Center, where he remembers making a stop and getting free orange juice while traveling on his sixth birthday with his parents. To my delight, they still offered this! John and I toasted his milestone birthday with orange juice in small paper cups.

It was wonderful.

It's "Me," Moma

It is now Saturday morning. We arrived late last night and are staying in a hotel close by to Moma. We have been updating her along our way. The idea of us coming was met with "absolutely NOT" at first. John made me realize that our presence is not welcome for a couple of reasons. First, she is very private. For all intents and purposes, my being there will disrupt her "routine." Our relationship has become long-distance, as visiting with her at home upsets her. Secondly, she protects and hides her dementia from sight. Our visit will be an intrusion and make her feel vulnerable.

Time draws closer, and I keep trying to make light of "seeing" her real soon.

During the morning, driving to her home, I was both excited and petrified at the same time. I had called her to let her know I was on my way. I'd be bringing two cat toys for Nayla, hoping she likes them—and ME, as she isn't used to having anyone else around. My stomach was filled with butterflies of excitement and nerves. I knocked on her door.

"Hi. You can't come in, as I'm dressed to head out for Walmart before it rains." She started to close the door. I lowered my voice to a whisper, so as not to startle her, and said, "It's me, Moma, Rene."

From then I watched as she searched my face for familiarity. She said I looked like one of her sisters. As she continued blocking the doorway, I asked if I could come in.

She waited a bit and then said yes.

Our Visit

I hugged her gently, as she's a little bit of a thing, and sat down in the kitchen with her. She was still trying to place me, saying I do look familiar. I calmly kept reassuring her who I am. She went along with everything and even took me on her porch to show me her favorite trees in the back. I could tell she still couldn't place me completely. After all, my voice has been her daughter and "caregiver" on the phone from Boston. She has been overly protective of her privacy these past few years, as if it was her only proof of independence. She has no memory that I, too, lived in this house. She showed me what was my old room and motioned to my two guitars in the corner. "I don't know who plays, but I have two guitars." I am a stranger to her, yet she was being very polite and showing me around. My heart was breaking as I watched her. It was very hard to know that she didn't feel my presence, but as painful as it was, it was not hurtful—as I knew she couldn't help it.

After a while, I left, letting her know that I would return with my husband, John, soon. A quick "Thank you" from Moma, and I was off to the hotel.

Funny, I didn't cry this day. I will later.

One Step at a Time

We picked Moma up for her appointment. John drove, I sat in the back, and Moma, in the front. She still seemed a bit unsure of who we are, but some inner familiarity caused her to trust us. I helped her undress and redress for her X-ray. She kept thanking me. I feel good watching over her and helping. She seems so tiny, yet not frail; still the strong woman I remember. Afterwards, we stopped at Arby's on the way home. She is quite aware of her surroundings, even though she hasn't driven in years. She gave directions to John, where to turn to head home. I walked her upstairs and said I would call her later that night. I got a hug, which gives me strength to go on.

Our Time Together

I called her that evening, and she shared with me her day. She remembered going in the car and into a doctor's office.

She then told me of a nice woman who helped her at the office. I reminded her it was me. She took in the information, but it didn't register—until the next morning when I called to say hello.

She began crying hysterically, asking if it was me yesterday that she remembers. I happily said yes. This upset her, as she thought we had left Florida and she had missed the opportunity to be with me "knowingly." I assured her we were only minutes away and would love to come by later today. This made her happy.

It still bothered her that she didn't recognize me and felt it must have hurt me. Rather than explaining the full theory of her recognizing my voice on the phone, rather than in person, I merely said to her, "I've gotten fat over the years, so why would you?" This made her laugh :-)

John and I took her to the "mother Walmart" and had such a wonderful time buying jeans for her and two matching clocks, one for her and one for us, symbolizing our "time together." It was priceless.

Doctor Visit

Monday morning was time to see her primary. While sitting in the office, I broached the subject of a caregiver again, to which she became so upset that she walked away from me in the sitting room. She returned a bit later but had dropped that subject completely. Not realizing that the caregiver would be a benefit for errands vs. using the bus—she still fights the idea. With some sound reasons.

"What are they going to do for me that I can't do myself? I need the housework to keep busy and the walk to Walmart for exercise. You would be taking that away from me. Not to mention the cost!"

A valid argument, if you think about it. But what options do I have really? She will, soon enough, be needing some assistance other than mine.

The doctor's visit went very well, as Moma's X-ray showed only arthritis and an old stress fracture, both of which are common at her age with her activity level. This was the first time I had met Moma's doctor in person. What a gentle man to match his caring voice. We have communicated via phone and text for years now. Boy, did I need him today.

I quickly brought him up to date regarding her "overly involved" neighbors and how they feel I should remove her from her home at this point. They have begun to harass both my mom and me after giving them a key to enter as needed. Though I do appreciate any "help," they go so far as bossing and scolding Moma when they feel it's needed. Point in case, she was wearing her sweater one day with it being quite warm in her home. The neighbor lowered the temperature and removed her sweater while scolding her of the warmth in the house—as if she had no thought for herself at all. This caused Moma to become angry and cry—followed by a phone call from her neighbor, insisting that I make her do the right thing. I did the right thing—I asked the neighbor to back off.

I had discussed with the doctor about preparing Moma to accept some help. He agreed and proceeded to explain to her that the time would come when assistance to oversee things would make her life easier. She didn't like his words any better than mine. He kept strong and steady to her arguments and frustration, explaining that we were trying to protect her freedom to live alone. Ironic, the one thing she felt was invading her privacy was going to help protect it.

She finally agreed to assistance, under duress, and the visit ended. Her argument, however, did not.

Assistance

After MANY calls to various places regarding home care, I found someone who seemed to fit the need perfectly. Moma, still fighting me, agreed to meet with her. The meeting went well but still an issue for Moma, due to her invasion of privacy and costs. I tried to say that it was covered under Medicare, but that didn't fly. She can be very lucid when she puts her mind to it. Makes it hard to negotiate with her.

Moma asked for some time to settle back into her life after this whirlwind since her fall. The doctor gave her a clean bill of health. She just wants to be left alone to regain her feelings of strength, normalcy, and independence.

I agreed for now.

Safety Lock

We were on our way to dinner, and Moma wasn't answering either phone. We had not said good night. Of course, I became worried, which is what I do best.

We were meeting friends who happened to be down in the area at the same time as us. Calling them to say we would be late, we headed over to Moma's home to check on her.

As we drove, I felt privileged to be so close that I needn't call anyone for help. Of course, I also got more nervous by the mile. We arrived at her home, and I knocked on the door. I used my key, only to realize her safety lock was on. Made me feel good that she indeed went to bed, as this is the last thing she does at night.

She came to the door half asleep and perfectly fine. Silly me. I offered to help her back to bed, but she explained to me, "Who would put the safety lock on?"

Good point—and she's the one with dementia.

Rather Be Known— Than Remembered

I brought apple turnovers to Moma—we sat in the kitchen and had a party. The day before, I stopped at Publix and bought fudge cookies and root beer. Moma can afford the weight. Me, not so much.

We did a walk through her home, with her asking if there was anything I could use to take back up North. Walking through my old room was a blast from the past. Everything was as I had left it many years ago.

She was trying to show me everything at once and said, "I don't know who played guitar, but there are two there. Would you like them?" She had shown them to me before. This time I quietly said, "Me, Moma, it's me who plays." Then came a painting of mine, one of many. She didn't remember that I paint. Nor did she remember the chess sets were mine. I sat on the floor at the end of the bed and reminded her that I was her "Little" Rene—her response was, "Of course, I know you are," with a big smile.

Moma was beginning to know who I am but had lapses as to who I was. Seeing me in front of her, she mostly accepted that I was her daughter. She had no connection, however, to my past with her or who I was. I reached for her hand and was grateful to be, at least in the moment, with her … for now.

Today was the day I cried.

On my drive back to our hotel, I realized I would rather be "known" than "remembered" … and I smiled.

Leaving to Return

We were planning for three or four days in Florida. For every day we stayed longer (twelve total), joy filled our hearts. I knew it would be hard to leave. I had always said that when I go down to Florida, it would be to bring Moma back with me, as I wouldn't want to leave her.

It was so true.

The day we chose to head back, we went to see Moma, who met us downstairs and pretty much tried to keep us from going up. She didn't want it to be emotional or for us to find it hard to leave. She kept it simple and fun by bringing more things to the car for our return home. Almost like seeing your kids off to college. In hindsight, it was brilliant. Such a motherly thing to do. Moma used to always say that I had to leave before I could come back. "You'll be back in one minute." This became our mantra every time I went to visit them. Pictures were taken and long-lasting hugs were given. As I said, "I love you more," she responded, "I love you forever."

I cry even now.

The next morning, we headed back North. I drove to stay focused. I managed to drive from Boynton Beach, where our hotel was, to Lake Worth Pier and had to pull over. I had just experienced the second hardest day ever—first, arriving to Moma not knowing who I was ... and then having to leave Moma when she does. John and I sat in the lot while I called her. She made me feel good, as she always can, by reminding me I was on my way back so I could start my return.

With each mile we drove, as hard as it was, I was that much closer to "returning."

*My gift to Moma and Daddy for their fiftieth wedding anniversary—
an acrylic painting I did depicting a stone bridge that symbolizes the strength
of their love and union, night and day throughout all the seasons.
The elements for a strong, solid foundation are all here—air, water, and earth.*

Our Rainbow

○○○✦○○○

On our way back to Boston, we saw a rainbow during one of my calls with Moma.

"We will be back in one minute, Moma." Thank you, God.

Moma's first and second parts of her four-part "I love you," 2016.

Wonderful

Our journey began July 9th. We returned home the night of the 28th. We traveled 20 days. It seemed like a lifetime yet flashes before my eyes in a moment. It was laughter. It was sadness. Aches and pains followed by dancing hearts. It was all new yet somehow familiar. Learning our dance of the day together.

It was wonderful.

Moma's third and fourth parts of her four-part "I love you," 2016.

Moma and me.

Part 9
Back in Rhythm

August 2014 – August 2014

Moma's Saigon, Vietnam, identification card in 1967.

Lesson Learned

Back from our trip from seeing Moma, I am still filled with every emotion possible. I'm settling back into the current daily issues, while trying to apply any new knowledge I might have learned. Listen more, say less. An old lesson from ages ago that most people, myself included, have yet to master.

Today Moma told me she lost her spare key. I had helped her bury it in the usual spot before we left from Florida. With her on the cell phone, I virtually went to the hidden spot and helped her dig up where the key should be. No key was found. She kept saying that she dug the key up and cleaned it, which she did while I was there. I figured this was her memory and not current. Where then might it be?

Confusion set in with Moma, as it does with any drama. I think of it as a mechanism that shuts us down at the time we lose control of a situation. Brilliant, if you think about it. Of course, the issue at hand is still there. Unable to make spare keys from her master key due to her missing owner's key card, my thought is to replace her lock. I find a local locksmith—now the issue of multiple keys to be made.

I think of calling in the assistant Moma met with during our trip. Sadly, I "thought out load," which caused Moma to state that the assistant hadn't been around, even though she was paid for the month. Of course, I reminded her that there had been no payment as yet, due to no service per my request. But when Moma's mind is busy, she will only hear herself, over and over again. Expected really, so why then did I believe there would be any other outcome than the one that happened?

I was the stimuli for this issue today. Yet, I became upset with the illness that has been given to my mom. For this, I handled things poorly and made us both sad. I apologized to Moma, who continued to be the stable one in the conversation.

After some time passed, I called her back to say I love you. She had forgotten what the issue was all about. I laughed at myself for crying and carrying the burden of my reaction today.

All that said, I will try from now on to say less and only share things as needed that might confuse her.

Lesson learned.

What to Do with Keys

Changing the lock now accomplished, I breathe a sigh of relief. The confusion behind us, we can no doubt move on. I had six keys made for her. Now came the daunting task of determining who gets the keys.

I have yet to receive them, though I believe there are two on their way to John and me. The master key is worn by Moma. That should leave three keys.

A big to-do about these keys. For starters, they had been accounted for and placed "somewhere." Trying to help verbally find the keys, Moma enlightened me that some are silver, while others are gold and they differ in shape. Could she be confusing the old key with the new? No, they all work, but how? Surely this is impossible, and I need to help guide her back to viewing only the new keys.

Round and round we go. Only to have it dawn on me that the new lock would have come with two original keys, while the copies could, no doubt, be a different shape and color from these. Thank goodness I figured it out—I had become part of the problem again, believing it was a dementia issue. I really need to stop that, LOL.

Finally, we buried one key again and secured two with neighbors. Problem solved.

Silver Alert

I am upset with how my demeanor has changed. Where is my patience and the sharpness to these issues that have shaped our lives the past four-plus years?

This was the first time I've seen Moma since the diagnosis. I had already felt the reality check of changes in our daily lives. I even re-read the beginning of our journal to view our journey from the beginning. I definitely experienced all the cliché stages expected. Why then now, do I feel overwhelmed with anxiety?

It dawned on me that after spending wonderful time with Moma and returning home to Boston, I have now witnessed her dementia firsthand and "feel" the changes physically that I have been experiencing for years only verbally on the phone. It was as if I needed to post a Silver Alert. Someone came and "kidnapped" my mom. Though it all made perfect sense, the stark reality hit me after our return. Panic swept in, then a brief time of anger for this illness. Lastly, I reached for John's steady hand and moved on toward the next step.

I realize the feelings now, and I'm embracing them as part of the process. It's in embracing that we can accept, release, and return to our "normal" chaotic journey of dementia.

Mind's Eye

I remember one time Moma was in her garden with a water bucket and shovel. I called to say hi and found her in a quandary. Seemed she was unable to remove the shovel from the watering can after it slipped in by accident. She would reach in and pull, shake, and even resort to a few select words but alas, nothing.

I suggested she reach her hand in and take hold of the shovel by the end of the handle. Then carefully lift the shovel by the handle and pull it straight up and out.

She was amazed and asked how I could manage this so quickly and over the phone. "Magic," she said. Not at all.

You see, if you become too close to an issue, your mind becomes anxious and without reason. This caused Moma's dementia to be clouded even further over this puzzling problem. I, on the other hand, not being faced with dementia and having the distinct advantage of being removed from the issue, could view it in my "mind's eye." Moma was trying to pull the shovel out the top of the watering can while keeping it flat (horizontal), hence causing a gridlock every time. Her dementia, along with the closeness to the issue, left her overwhelmed.

I wish during our quandaries, we were always grounded enough to close our eyes and view the problem with our mind's eye for clarity every time.

Funny, to think that with our eyes closed—sometimes we can see more clearly.

Dementia in the Forefront

I woke today with the clarity of anxiety, confusion, and frustration. Sound like an oxymoron? Maybe so. But along with my own anxiety of late, I have noticed Moma to be somewhat hyper and combative, with the latter happening a little more frequently.

Truth be told, the past few weeks have taken their toll on us all. I have shared *my* feelings on paper. Let me now express what I believe Moma is feeling.

Her tranquil surroundings took a major turn after her fall from the ladder. Her neighbors invaded her space. A stranger in the form of a social worker, called by her neighbor, came uninvited to assess her. Moma passed with flying colors, thank God. Then, I showed up at her door. In hindsight, no wonder her head is spinning.

Realizing her dementia at the forefront of her days, is it any wonder that she feels the need to be combative? Even a wild animal's instinct is to strike for protection if they feel vulnerable. Sadly, Moma is quite aware of her mental changes and indeed feels vulnerable.

I need to find a way of communicating with her without emotion showing in my voice. Stay neutral, if you will—respond without personal tone. But how is this accomplished when it *is* personal? Even for the nonfamily caregiver, it can feel somewhat personal. After all, a lot of time and effort is invested in trying to make a difference, trying to keep your family member or patient safe and happy. No one likes to feel their efforts to be futile. Truth is, nothing given in love is ever futile—but we must realize, as caregivers, that our efforts must be very fluid and change on the spot as needed, without letting it be personal.

Though I, too, am a victim, along with Moma, of her dementia, she, after all, is the one living the change. I am merely experiencing it. May I say this is easier said than done. Stay strong.

Part 10
Life Is All Things

August 2014 – October 2014

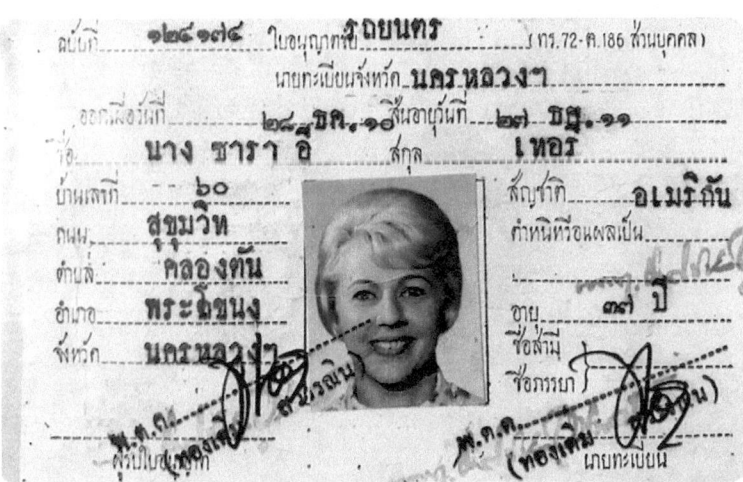

Moma's Thailand identification card in 1968.

24-Hour Day

These past few days have been like old times. Moma always said to me that if I wanted a situation to change, it had to start with me. It was up to me to view the situation in a new light that would make it seem less troubling, even turning it into something good.

I can't say there is anything good about dementia. What I can say is that it's up to us to find some joy in every day. I lost sight of that because of the fast pace of the past two months. Now, with time to breathe, I feel the peace that comes with the mundane beauty of life.

To complete a 24-hour day, there is darkness and light. Rejoice the day—enjoy your night. It takes both to complete your life.

Loving Both

A dear friend of mine was discussing how dementia changes our loved ones. She too, experienced the life-altering trauma of dementia with her mother. She said something that stuck with me.

"Find and enjoy a relationship with who your mom is now and know that the mom you remember is still inside of her. When the time comes for her to join Heaven, she will take both the current mom that you have learned to love and the mom that you always loved with her. You will have been a part of both."

Amen.

The Question

I often felt over the years that when Moma would ask the same question repeatedly, it was up to me to find various ways to respond, understanding that she cannot retain new information. Maybe with different words in the answer, it would stick.

I read daily about dementia. I find comfort and strength in the stories I find online and knowledge in any articles I read. I found a statement the other day that switched on a light. It said that people with dementia don't ask the same thing repeatedly because they don't remember the answer, they ask repeatedly because they don't remember asking the question.

I get it now.

Calamine Lotion

Let's talk calamine lotion for a bit. For months now, Moma has been saying that she swears by calamine lotion for her bruises. Being that her skin is on the thin side, due to her age, the slightest bump causes bruising on her. Out comes her calamine lotion to be slathered all over like a wonder drug. While describing to me the miracle of it all, she calmly reminded me that it will take anywhere from seven to ten days for the bruises to fade, of course. "Of course." And let's remind ourselves that it will usually take seven to ten days for bruises to fade on their own.

Not to burst Moma's bubble, I always say that I am taking notes on this wonder drug. Truth be told, one time while hearing her news yet again, I googled calamine for bruises. NO words to explain my surprise of the result that zinc in the lotion actually does help bruises.

Speechless and "eating my thoughts."

Presidential Speech

One day, while solving the problems of the world, Moma surprised me with a statement that even now I find hard not to giggle at. After her spirited speech on whatever subject we were discussing, I said to her, "You got it going on, Moma!" In a very calm and direct tone she replied, "Yeah, I am practicing my presidential speech. How'd I do?" We both laughed.

You're doing great, Moma. Doing great!!

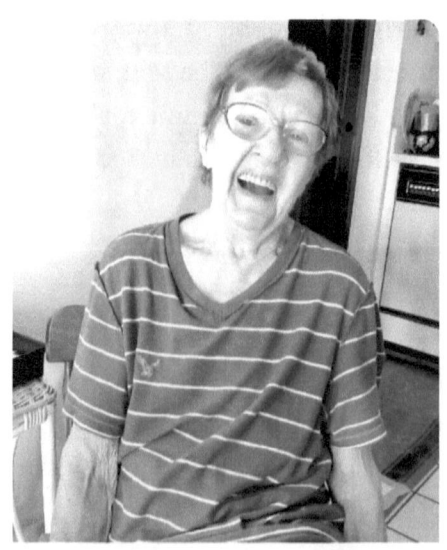

Tiny Sparrow

This morning I noticed a tiny sparrow—high up on a limb of a pine tree in our back yard. It was quite breezy, yet he didn't try to fly further into the branches for protection. At first, I thought him to be a baby, playing with the winds and choosing to hold on for fun. But soon it dawned on me that he was waiting for a break in the wind.

See, if he tried to fly during the gust of wind, he would likely lose his balance and be tossed around. Rather, by waiting for the right time, he could use the wind to help guide him to safety and carry on with his day.

I realized we could all learn from this sparrow. When things are at their worst, I find myself scurrying around in the "gusty winds," trying to make things right. Like a bird in the swirling winds, I am tossed around and usually find no safe landing during the gusts. Yet, if I wait for things to settle a bit in both my life and mind, I can then see more clearly how to "fly" through the issues and find safe passage.

Timing is everything. Leave it to one of God's creatures to make it so simple.

Part 11
Thankfulness

November 2014 – January 2015

Moma in 1969, age 39.

Partners

Thanksgiving is a time to reflect and be thankful for the blessings in our lives. This year is extra special, as so much has happened in the past few months. The most precious of all was our visit to Moma this summer.

During our trip, everything happened so fast. Emotions were reeling. Happiness, sadness, confusion, joy, closeness—closeness of Moma and me. Closeness beyond being mother and daughter and best friends, but now also making the feeling of caregiver as real as ever. I have been caring for Moma since the onset of her dementia, only now, it became tangible—I felt like her caregiver. We have become care "partners"… because you see, though I may be caring for my mom's needs, all the while she is making me a better person. I am learning so much about life and myself. I am blessed to be sharing this time with her.

With that said, this year I am especially thankful for my mom and the blessing of our relationship. I am also blessed to have my husband, John, sharing every step along the way—sometimes holding me up and other times… holding my hand.

Thank you, God.

Coins

December 2014

Something is lost every day. It can be tangible, like a sweater. It can be found, like your misplaced car keys. Or it can be part of your past.

Moma and I have been exchanging coins for years now to be placed in our windowsill New Year's Eve. This custom was shared by a co-worker; a tradition of exchanging one penny, nickel, dime, and quarter and then placing them together in the corner of your windowsill. This was to bring you prosperity, insuring you "enough" to keep you well the following year. Every December we would mail each other our coins and place them in the windows together.

Every December—but this one.

I started early in the month reminding "us both" to prepare our coins. In preparing her coins, Moma became confused as to whether or not she had posted them. I suggested she send another set just in case. This too became confusing. She did receive my coins but couldn't fully understand the meaning or purpose. I realized then that this part of our history had been lost to her dementia.

I cry even now at the loss, as it is hard to watch pieces of your life with someone so dear leave you. It's scary, actually.

I managed to have Moma place my coins in her window. I never did receive her coins in the mail, though I didn't let her know. Instead, I had John hand me coins that I placed in our corner window. We managed to complete the tradition together.

Somehow, I felt we saved the ritual, at least for this year.

Quarter Pound

With something lost, you must look for something found. For Moma, this year it is the deli at her local Walmart. I tried for some time to get her to stop at the deli. One day, as she was in line to be serviced, I called there and asked if someone would give special handling to her. The deli relationship was born. She now enjoys more variety and says she feels like she's ordering out.

I learned something during this find. I learned to think "dementia" when speaking with Moma. When discussing how to purchase items at the deli, I was recommending she buy a quarter of a pound until she knew she liked it. This way she could test everything. With a fourth of a pound, you don't waste it. I noticed that she was having a hard time grasping how much to purchase. No matter how many times I repeated it, she was confused.

Can you find the problem? My wording of "quarter of a pound" swapped with "fourth of a pound." Two versions of the same meaning. It became clear as a bell. Once I stuck with the wording "fourth of a pound," everything fell into place.

Today Moma chose to purchase a half a pound all on her own because she liked it so much.

Wondrous.

Part 12
Time of Whirlwind

❧

January 31, 2015 – February 25, 2015

Moma with her favorite sunflowers in Thailand in 1970, age 40.

The Fall

Many days have passed since I put life to paper. Last visit was January 20 at 3:55 in the afternoon. Who knew that 11 days, almost to the hour, our lives would change? Change. Six letters that can turn your life upside down. One word—packed with every emotion imaginable. I begin my visit today from January 31, 2015. Let's do this.

Moma was in her marketplace Walmart having a wonderful time. I called her, as I always do, and caught her in the aisle of cat food. Happy, carefree, almost ready to check out with her chocolate and head back home. I was out shopping and called John next. Once he realized that I was safely in my car, he shared with me the news.

Greenacres Police had called our home. Moma was walking home and steps away from her condo when the neighbor backed his car into her, knocking her over onto the pavement. I pause, even now, remembering the feeling of these words overwhelming me. My heart stopped. I became numb. John's words finally pierced my thoughts again, and I heard that she was okay and on her way by ambulance to JFK Hospital, thank God.

Breathe.

Finding the number on my phone, I called the hospital, asking about Moma. Registration hadn't been updated as yet, so there was no record of her. I called her cell as a last option and to my delight, she answered. My world began moving again. She went on to tell me she was fine, and they were examining her. She sounded so good—my heart smiled.

Thank you, God.

Nights at JFK Hospital

Moma spent 12 hours in emergency. X-rays showed a fractured pelvis along with scrapes and cuts on her left elbow and leg. Panic is an understatement, as the mileage between us became more apparent. Speaking with the triage nurse, updating any medical information they might need, and hearing that she was doing well kept my sanity. Deciding to admit her due to the fracture, she was put in a room after a very long wait. This would prove to be a pivotal moment in the decline of her dementia, with the traumatic recovery of her accident.

Dementia robs you of understanding change. She has now been in emergency with endless tests and was in a hospital room without Nayla, with no familiar surroundings, and being told she mustn't move due to her injury. None of this made sense to her, even with my trying to explain the need to follow medical directions.

Moma spent three days and two nights in that hospital. It was maddening. Stuck in Boston with our snowiest year on record, Moma was going through hell with confusion, pain pills, and trauma, while I was unable to get on a flight, due to cancellations causing overbookings. Even Amtrak was compromised with the snowy tracks. On her second night, she was moved to a monitored room, as she didn't understand the need to remain in bed and kept trying to get up. For her dementia, she was now two rooms for two nights, creating even more confusion to her life. Though I was in constant contact with the doctors and nurses' station, I found a few were considerate of her special needs while most treated us both as one of many patients in their day. I believe some have forgotten what it feels like to be the patient—sadly.

Transfer

Now into our third day in the hospital, Moma was experiencing hallucinations from the pain medication they were keeping her on. Percocet was needed for her pain level and to keep her from trying to walk to the bathroom alone. Her dementia was in full bloom. She felt they were keeping her captive and became angry with me that I was allowing this to happen. I tried to keep her stable by calling all hours of the day, reassuring her everything was going to be okay and that she was safe. It tore my heart out to be so far away from her.

On this day, Moma was transferred into a rehab center that I found through her insurance company. There was so much going on that I had to keep a running ledger of names and numbers for follow-up and to keep things happening behind the scene. Moma's neighbors were assisting with Nayla while I was planning her recovery.

The next phase had begun.

Recovery Begins

The rehab was nice enough. One of Moma's neighbors had her husband there on the resident dementia floor.

It was great to have someone we knew arrive there every day—though Moma rarely recognized her. Gege, Moma's pharmacist, went to visit her and took a picture of them while there. Words can't explain how great it was to see her, if only in a picture.

Everything was an issue, right down to her wanting to "lock up" for the night and trying to close her door. It upset her so much to sleep with the door open. She "feared Nayla would get out." Not understanding her surroundings, she would become angry with me that I, again, was allowing this to happen to her. On occasions, she would have a roommate. They would draw the curtain for her privacy, which led her to think they were "hiding her." She was always alarmed she hadn't paid her bill.

I tried endlessly to keep her calm, all the while losing my mind in Boston. The snow was still an issue for travel. I searched various ways out... even thought of driving again. Moma's caseworker spoke with me daily—each conversation ending with my question of "When can I take her home?" She kept reminding me that showing up prematurely would be a problem for Moma, as she would then fight to go home once seeing me. Instead, I needed to make her feel "at home" during this time to speed up her recovery. Though this made perfect sense, every part of me was falling apart.

Dark Days

Moma would spend two weeks in recovery. Fourteen days of repetitive confusion and frustration. One of the hardest times in our days was therapy early afternoon and yet another PT later that day. It used to be an issue for her that she had no schedule, but rather they would come and get her random times. This made her nervous, thinking she wouldn't be "ready" when they arrived for her. Each morning she would ask me her schedule for the day. I would try to make it seem as normal as possible, trying to find ANYTHING good about her stay in the rehab. Anything at all.

She would repeatedly ask about Nayla. I would explain again that her neighbor was watching over her. Other neighbors would bring her food, chocolate, and even clothes. It was wonderful that friends stepped up and showed concern. We were in constant communication. Me—updating them on her progress and they, advising me of how she looked, sometimes sending pictures of her in bed. It made my heart happy to feel closer somehow.

There were moments of Moma accepting her surroundings. I would talk with her about her "room" away from home, trying to help her with any recognition of her day. After therapy, I would start in on describing her bed or dresser, from the pictures I had been sent, to pull in any familiarity, any constant, any comfort. The nurses' faces would change daily by the shift. Her physical therapists would change, depending on their days off. So even during her recovery, there was no consistency to grasp onto. Nothing at all.

Confusion of what had happened, overwhelming feelings of the pain and recovery, and dumbfounded fear of what was to come had become her "norm." Sadly, she even began to forget her own home, believing Nayla was there with her and they lived in that room. She was randomly aware of her dementia, which led her even more to believe she was in a "home" for people with the illness. I had faith, with time, things would get better. Problem with time—it takes time. Long, agonizing time. My heart was breaking.

Moma's Bed

Somehow things began to come together. Having been in daily communication with her case manager from the rehab, I had finally gotten clearance to take Moma home. I discussed the repercussions of her remaining in the facility while her mind was losing more memory every day. Continuing her therapy at home would allow me to help her regain her memory of Nayla and her home, which would help in the overall recovery. Medically, the doctor cleared her, and I was free to take her home the upcoming Monday.

Snow was still an issue. The season broke our previous record on file. We ended up getting just over 108 inches, most of which fell in the months of January and February, allowing no time for removal between storms and no place to put all the snow. The city used snow melting machines to dispose of the piles, only for two more piles to be delivered. The flights were endlessly full due to cancellations. The roads were difficult to navigate. The trains and buses were having issues too.

A snowy Friday the 13th night—flights overbooked, fearing I would be unable to make connections on Delta as an employee, I purchased an employee discount standby ticket on JetBlue nonstop. There were no confirmed tickets for sale, as the seats were filled with passengers bumped from cancelled flights. I had John take me to the airport with little assurance I would get on. First flight, all passengers showed, and I failed. Waiting another hour for the next flight, God saw fit to have one person no-show, and I was on! Elated, I called John and cried.

I had said good night to Moma earlier in the evening, with no mention of the flight, being unsure if I would indeed make it. John got on the phone and booked a car rental for me. He asked Moma's neighbor to leave a light on for my arrival. After all was done, I was in the house about 11:30 PM. Exhausted, overwhelmed, grateful, I called John, checked on Nayla, and fell asleep in Moma's bed.

Finally.

Happy Heart

I awoke the following morning and called Moma. I told her that I am in Florida at her condo with Nayla, who is doing well. I said that I would be coming to see her in about 30 minutes, to which she seemed very happy and confused at the same time. After getting my bearings, I set out to find her rehab after stopping for flowers at her Walmart.

    I can't wait to see her.

Are You My Rene?

Seeing Moma that first moment was joyous. She looked so small in that big bed, surrounded by her teeth, glasses, and cell phone. There was a yellow notepad on her nightstand with answers to herself about repeated concerns. I found that heartwarming. I knew she was safe and being taken care of—but I couldn't wait to take her home.

Of course, this was only Saturday, and I wasn't able to take her home until Monday. I knew this could present a problem, but I was so ready to be with her and watch over her... along with the fear of more snow that weekend, which gave me reason to go at this time.

She woke from her nap and saw my face. Tears of joy filled her eyes. I couldn't stop holding her. She seemed so tiny, fragile yet still "in control." My heart was overwhelmed with joy to be near her.

During my first day there, I spent the time with Moma sharing lunch and dinner, answering any questions about Nayla, and showing her pictures of her home. Her memory of "home" had faded after being away for two weeks. I had taken pictures when John and I were there last July. I took my iPad and showed her every one in full detail, hoping to prepare her memory for her return home. At first, they were vaguely familiar but soon became more so.

There were the many times, that due to my being present and assisting her to the bathroom or with sitting up in bed, she would ask me how long I had been working at the rehab. She didn't recognize me as her daughter at those times, but rather a caregiver helping her. At first, this broke my heart...but then I realized that she had never been in this position before and had been taken care of for two weeks by nurses...I just became one of them.

I would gently remind her that I was her daughter, Rene. She would clear her eyes and focus in on my face and say, "Are you MY Rene?"

I would smile and say, "Yes, Moma," and we would hug again as if for the first time.

Homeward Bound

I split my time between staying with Moma at rehab and out buying equipment to prepare her home for her arrival: handicapped toilets, bed bar, all medications and foods. I would have breakfast, lunch, and dinner with her, followed by a bit of TV, and then put her to bed until the morning.

Monday finally came, and this was the day to take her home. Trying to jar her memory, we spent lots of time looking at the photos of Nayla and her home again. More paperwork and lots of red tape—we were finally free to return home. It felt amazing.

A place that should be familiar and comforting. A place to feel secure and happy. I turned the key and prayed to God that these emotions would return.

The Reunion

First steps in—so important. How much do you guide her? Truth is, the fact that I was even present kept the moment from being the norm. I chose to back away after setting her up in the living room, hoping that Nayla would come to her. This would be the beginning.

Nayla was overjoyed to see Moma. During all this trauma, Nayla was deeply involved as well. She might have even witnessed the accident and, no doubt, saw the commotion of the ambulance, as it was just outside her window. She had been waiting for Moma's return from Walmart that fateful day. Time must have dragged, and abandonment might have entered her mind. The whole issue is tough to recount.

The reunion was joyous.

March 10, 1930, Birthdate

Amazingly, Moma stepped right into her old role of caring for Nayla and herself. She knew where the kitchen was, her bedroom, and recognized everything in her home. I became overconfident that the issue was behind us. Truth be told, the accident and rehab facility were behind us. Recovery was still alive and well ahead of us.

Moma was cleared for rehab to be continued at home. Prior to this, she had visits from the nurse to assure her recovery thus far. I can say that she wasn't happy about all this unwanted attention—but rather, now at home, wanted to be left alone. I gently explained this was required in order to allow returning home so soon.

She did well with the nurse, at several times even getting a bit fresh. The nurse asked general questions of clarity such as the year, the date... all of which Moma said, "Since I have no job, why would I know the date?" Okay... then she was asked her age, to which she gave her birthdate. When asked why, she directly said, "My age changes, my birthdate doesn't."

Amazing.

Slippery Slope

Rehab came rather easy. The therapist would come and do stretches and strengthening exercises, followed by occupational therapy. This would entail learning to walk with her walker and quad cane, and mastering the stairs again, since she lives upstairs. Because of her overall strong health, due to all her prior walking days, this went easily.

Thank God for anything easy.

Days went by and my presence was confusing to Moma. I understood completely, as the last time I lived at home was 27 years ago! I explained the need for my presence was due to bringing her home early from rehab. The requirement was that I stay with her for some time. This explanation bought me "some time."

I had to be careful at night, as when I would hear her up, my instinct was to check on her. Of course, my presence would startle her, which I then would feel bad about. There were times she would tell me all was well, and I was allowed to leave now. I realized she thought I was a visiting nurse and was hoping me "be gone." I would gently remind her it was me—and the need for my presence a bit longer. This worked "some" of the times.

Other times, not so good. She would become irate that I was accusing her of not knowing her own blood family. Slippery slope, as in her mind, she felt I was saying "she was losing it." After some time, she would begin to place my face, only then the guilt would come with her saying, "How could I not feel that you were my daughter?"

The whole thing was tough.

"In the Neighborhood"

One day I ran out to pick something up from Walmart. I explained what I was doing and when I would return.

I asked if she would like to go with me, but she wanted to stay home, if for no other reason but to get rid of me for a bit. I tried to make sure my outing wasn't later in the day, as this would be too close to sundowning (a symptom of dementia usually displayed as late-day confusion). I then called to advise I was on my way home. Even with what I thought was covering all bases, she was amazed that I was "in the neighborhood and wanted to drop by." Is it any wonder I kept my outings to a minimum?

One day, I walked down to a neighbor's home to deliver flowers. I gave flowers to all neighbors that helped Moma and me during this hard time. While there, forgetting the time of day being 6:30, Moma chose to close up for the night. I returned home some 10 minutes later to find the door locked and deadbolt on from the inside. Yes, I was locked out. I simply called her from my cell and said I was in the neighborhood.

She opened the door and we both laughed.

Good Moments

There were more times than not that she did realize my presence and who I was. Other times, she would have confusion of her schedule. She would wake in the morning only to think the nurses would be there any minute to bathe her. She hated that. An invasion of privacy and humiliating. I would remind her that we were home, and no one was allowed in her home without her permission. The days of that type of care were over. She was "in charge" of herself for bathing and feeding. This made her happy and stronger.

These moments were good.

John's Arms

After some two weeks, Moma was more than hinting that I should return home to John. She asked me if I was still married. I said yes, to which she replied, "Then go home." No subtleness here. I was having trouble determining when to leave—though her mental recovery was coming along well. I knew she needed her space but, oh my God, I just didn't want to let go.

I finally pulled myself together and got on a plane heading for home. It was unimaginably hard to leave her, though I knew she was at home there with Nayla and personal care. I remembered Moma saying I would always have to go home before I could head back.

Soon I was in John's arms. Thank you, God, for holding us all, and please don't ever let go.

Part 13
Moving On

March 2015 – June 2015

Moma and me at Wat Arun in Thailand, 1970.

New Chapter of Life

One would think that a hurdle was behind us now. Truth be told, the road laid out in front of us seemed endless. Moma had changed. Her mind was working differently.

She still knew where she was, but her confidence level had shifted. I soon realized that life as we knew it would never be the same.

"Doctor's" Orders

While home with Moma, I had worked on getting her a caregiver. Something she NEVER wanted before. I explained that walking to Walmart, as she had in the past, would be a bad idea, what with the recovery of her pelvic bone. I added that since her physical therapy had ended, her doctor requested to continue her healing by having outings in a controlled surrounding like Walmart or Goodwill; somewhere the weather and broken sidewalks wouldn't be an issue. Saying he wanted this recovery three times a week, giving her body a day off between and the weekend off, seemed to make sense to Moma. I was so very happy she was receptive. Of course, all of this came from me, though her doctor did agree. And of course, all will be paid by her insurance. "Of course..."

Little white lies are allowed when keeping her safe. If she knew the truth, she would debate the issue, saying she wasn't in need of this service. Instead, it's "free"... paid for by her insurance to enjoy.

Shhhhhhh.

Something Good

Getting Moma to accept a caregiver was a blessing to me, as now I would have a point person, not only to take care of such things as filling her pills and taking her to appointments or the bank, but also Walmart—all without the need of the Palm Tran Connection. The fact that she could now be taken to Goodwill and thrift shops throughout the week enriches her life. It's as if she has returned to her old times with Betsy, going where she pleases. Makes me sooooo happy.

I also love the fact that I can ask for assistance to do odds and ends like change a light bulb or check her thermostat. I have them check on her needs around the house without involving her neighbors. She would have never allowed this before. Since this is due to her injury and being requested by "her doctor," it is becoming a reality.

Thank you, God, for any good that comes from something bad.

Moma at Goodwill, 2016.

Monday, Wednesday, Friday

It is amazing to think of an elderly person having to address all the paperwork that follows an accident. I have created a folder with all names and numbers, along with the dates I spoke to all affiliates. Hospital, ambulance, doctors, rehab, X-rays, bloodwork, medications, receipts of all items required for her home. It is a full-time job.

I am dealing with Humana and the insurance adjuster of the accident; payments made on my credit card, partial reimbursement checks issued, keeping track of what is owed and paid. It's overwhelming, while all the time trying to deal with the recovery, changes in Moma's mental status, the new normal in her everyday life, and life in general. Thank God Moma is being spared from this.

All she needs to know is if it's Monday, Wednesday, or Friday, go-out days with her caregiver. Priorities.

Hiding "Mistakes"

I have been noticing the shift in Moma's mental status still affecting her. She allows me to call her every day at 9 AM to take her pills, which is a wonderful thing. What a great relief for me. On the other hand, I can tell her confidence level is still jarred. She questions herself on almost everything, which in turn drives her mad. She is aware of this fact and tries to hide it from me, so she doesn't seem confused. She is misplacing things more often now. House keys, mailbox keys, and now her wallet. I had extra keys made and gave them to her caregiver. Of course, she found all keys in good time. Still missing the wallet. Problem is she doesn't release the feeling of having done something "wrong." Worse yet, "Rene" is aware of it. I have become the parent she keeps things from, feeling I have to "fix all her mistakes." Her words of course, though true feelings in her mind…causing her to want to hide even more from me.

Not good.

Embrace the Bumps

Moma's days all flow together, causing her mind to "blend" issues. Last week—misplaced keys, followed by wallet, and now money. Yes, money. It becomes all intertwined. She will call me and say, "I found my house key... all is well," when, in fact, that was last week's issue, and finding cash would be great now.

Last week she withdrew money from the bank Monday, Thursday, and again on Friday, as she kept misplacing it. All the time, she was extremely irate with me because she knew that I was aware of this. She feels her vulnerability as a liability and fears she is losing what independence she has left. It is a horrible situation.

I explain over and over again that all will be well, as the cash is somewhere in her home. However, on day three, I did say that we needed to make a plan to help her from misplacing the cash, which in turn causes her endless frustration.

Of course, this statement, in turn, caused her endless frustration...

I can say that this week has been the worst irate situation from Moma so far. I see new shifts in her personality. I do understand this is to be expected. It still hurts, though, and takes you—for some stupid reason—by surprise. I feel scared of losing her trust, which is needed greatly at this stage of caregiving.

I find that Moma trusts me but doesn't want to be vulnerable with me. It is such a fine line. She knows what I do to help her and to keep her safe, yet she needs to feel somewhat in charge of her own life. I magnify anything good to keep her happy. I want and need her to be happy so desperately. I think every day...today will be a good day. For some reason, I am disappointed when it's not...even with understanding dementia. It is time to get over that and try to find some joy in every day regardless. I need to expect more bumps in the road in order to brace for and embrace them.

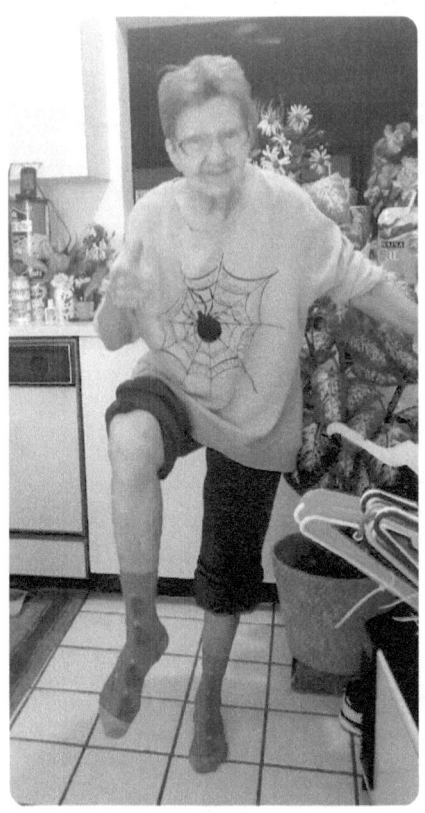

Losing Yourself

So today it all became clear.

Since the beginning of Moma's dementia, she chose to release her car, thus no more driving, she eventually released bill paying over to me, and she slowly accepted me making appointments and such. Through all this change, other than Moma feeling guilty "relying" on me, she was never angry about my help but rather appreciated it.

I made a promise to Moma years ago to always keep her safe with her dementia. My desire is to make her life as happy and healthy as possible, while living through the many webs of this disease. We try to find "normal" in every day.

Something we can touch or feel—something from who we were—to remind us who we still are.

This irate time of the past two weeks is a combination of things. I had to make a change by adding a caregiver, which brought on the swing of emotions, as anything new is not good. Confusion creeps in and things get misplaced. Feeling lack of control…and knowing that someone "knows" about it. Defiance, frustration, sadness. Oh yes, and now have your daughter take away the responsibility of your own money.

All new, alarming changes. Unwanted changes. Feeling like she is losing herself in full, broad view of life itself.

Part 14
Dear God

July 2015 – August 2015

Moma and me at Wat Arun in Thailand, 1970.

I'll Be Waiting

"I just need to have a conversation with you, God."
"WHY?"
"I have so many issues swirling around in my head."
"Pick one. Any one."
"Please get back to me. I'll be waiting."
"Thank you."

Moments of Memory

One thing that is so important to embrace when dealing with the madness of dementia—

"The best we can do is remember—we indeed still are and will always be us...no matter what."

I notice so many changes in Moma. Last month was my birthday. In the past, June was greeted each day with "Happy birthday month." One's birthday was always the most personal of all holidays celebrated in our family. All other holidays are shared with someone else. It was nice. It was constant. Sadly, it has been lost.

Now, one week before my birthday, Moma said to me, "Did you realize we are related?" Her epiphany was meant to be a happy realization.

It was.

She has made me promise to always remind her of anything important, with the reality that her dementia might get in the way. I reminded her of my birthday so she and I could sing "Happy Birthday" over the phone. I guess you can say that the love and feeling was still there, even with dementia—only now it happens in moments rather than memory.

"Moments of memory. That is dementia."

Hurting

Recently Moma was very combative for the most part of a day. Usually, I call her back a few hours later after her outburst and she has forgotten the issue. She has been holding onto the "feeling" of an outburst longer now. In the evening, I said to her that it had been a tough day for us both and explained we are going through this illness together. She is living and trying her best to survive it. I'm watching and feeling helpless. The whole situation is overwhelming.

Moma put her thoughts in one sentence that made me sit up and take notice. After I said that we had experienced a tough time, she calmly reminded me that when my day is a bad one with her, it is because she has been hurting that whole day. Wow.

What a realization. What a sadness.

Makes me love her even more.

Hell

Moma told me to go to hell today for the first time ever. I wish I could tell her we're already there.

Sadly, she remembered saying her words and called back to apologize. One would think this was appreciated, but in truth, it means to me that she is aware of her manners, and that saddens me even more. I realize that her words are hurtful but realize also that her words mean "she" is hurting.

So sad.

Two Potted Trees

Moma has been caring for two potted trees she found last month being tossed away. Seems she gave these trees away about five years ago and was glad to take them back, explaining to me how they have grown. All they need is love and care. She waters them and cleans the leaves daily.

Finding their height to be a bit tall for her porch, she carried them down to the corner garden of Park Pointe to set them up where they can get the rain and sun. They seem to be thriving there. Makes her happy.

They are artificial. Though the trunk is real, the leaves are not. I became aware of this a while back and never shared it with Moma. I didn't want to upset her reality.

It doesn't really matter that she is watering artificial plants; it makes her happy to care for them. We all should remember that one's reality may be different from another's. Reality is not just facts but also personal emotions and circumstances. If we could learn to accept realities other than our own, life would be simpler.

New Moves

Moma asked me the other day about her condition. She knows that something is not right but forgets on occasion that she has dementia. I gently reminded her that any confusion is due to her having dementia for over five years now. She was surprised and said, "I thought I was dancing pretty well."

I assured her that she is and replied that having dementia doesn't mean you stop dancing... it means you learn new moves.

Moma and I are learning a new dance daily. Please keep the music coming.

Misplaced Past

I have begun to notice that Moma has no conception of time, even more now. She will go out on a given morning with her caregiver, have a good time, and return home, only to ask if she will be going out tomorrow. I gently remind her that tomorrow is a "stay home day." To which she replies, "Two days in a row?" They say that dementia steels away your sense of time. It is quite noticeable now. For the most part, this doesn't seem to affect her terribly, but I am aware to respond carefully, as she will sometimes be frustrated by her lack of memory. When Moma forgets something, I see it as a piece of her past getting misplaced—she sees it as a scary hole where something once was. It breaks my heart. I wish for her that when she does forget, she would also "forget to care about it."

Mrs. Robert A. Torry

Pichai Court
177 Pichai Road   Phone 46468
Bangkok, Thailand   Apt. 403

นางโรเบิท เอ เทอรี่

หอพักพิชัย
177 ถนนพิชัย   โทร. 46468
พระนคร   ห้อง 403

Moma's Thailand ID card.

Part 15
Life Is...

August 2015 – October 2015

Moma in Thailand, 1970.

Heaven

M oma was just pondering about issues that were painful here on Earth and wondering how they will be in Heaven. I told her not to worry, for God takes over all problems as we enter His Kingdom, and we will have everything we need.

"Heaven comes fully furnished."

Moma with Dad and me in Thailand, 1970.

The Search

Recently I was on the phone with Moma, and we needed to find her cell phone. I called it using my cell and could hear the ringing in the background. She went from room to room looking for the sound. I listened to her talking and searching for her phone until she let out a loud laugh. The phone was in her left pocket all the time and was following her every move. Because she didn't reach down into her pocket, the sound was never reachable. In her moment of searching, she was relying on sight only. In truth, when we search for things in life, we must rely on all senses to find what we are looking for. We need to "see" with more than our eyes.

Life Is

Life is…

For a moment there, I thought I had a handle on this phrase. Truth be told, I "got" nothing. Life is complicated. It is joyous and heartbreaking. It is hard yet has moments of pure ease. Sometimes you find yourself running right toward it while other times you want to pull the cover over your head and get the day over with.

Some say, "life is what you make it," while others say, "everything is written in the master plan." I believe it is a bit of both. Life, in general, has its ebb and flow traditionally. We can plan for our lives, as we all should, to some extent, but all the while must be prepared for that unforeseen curve in the road.

"Life gets in the way of living" is my saying.

While planning your life, you might find one day you wake up and learn that your future is filled with issues far from understood. It's as if you switched the channel unintentionally and can't seem to go back.

Rest assured, you will eventually catch up with the new "plot" and find yourself beginning again with what we call "life."

Take a deep breath and enjoy.

Fractured Fairy Tale

Moma is always talking a blue streak about a subject that seems to be weaved together with other thoughts.

She tells it as if it just happened, from beginning to end, without missing a beat. Took me a while to learn how to dissect the story and learn what was what.

I was reading the other day and came across the words "fractured fairy tale." Seems a fractured fairy tale is a story that is well-known, only altered to make it your own. You will recognize familiar passages and think you know the next words, only with a fractured fairy tale, you never know what to expect.

With dementia, Moma will take various memories and put them together into a story line that seems as though it just happened. If you listen hard enough, you can hear the segments and see where they are being weaved together. Every part of her story comes from something real, only out of context. "My neighbors just left for four months overseas and borrowed my pliers."

Actually, her neighbor visited family stateside for a short time; Moma sent lots of her shirts to Haiti through her caregiver, Fafa; and takes four pills every morning. The pliers were misplaced, but her neighbors "borrowing" them validates why she can't find them. All real stuff. Nothing to do with each other.

Fascinating.

Fafa

Speaking of Fafa, this young lady is a godsend to our lives. Her full name is Wansaifla Geffrard. She is the niece of Gege, mentioned in previous chapters. She is 18 years old and already a nurse's assistant. Her studies in college are caregiving for the elderly.

She is loving, responsible, knowledgeable, and sent to us by the "Man" upstairs.

Really.

Moma considers her family, as do I. Because of her training, she understands and is considerate of her outbursts and knows how to defuse them. She is wonderful at handling any situation that may arise—as with dementia, you never really know what to expect. People speak of mood swings; with dementia, you experience "moment" swings. Every moment can bring another mood of agitation or happiness. The mind becomes stuck in fast-forward, and it is literally hard to keep up with your emotions.

As a caregiver, you need to be a special kind of person to stay on this roller coaster.

Fafa is one of those people.

Surely Joy Remains

There are times in a caregiver's life that dementia has the last word. For almost six years, I have stayed with any issue, always trying to make it right—to make Moma feel better. That is my main goal.

I have noticed that the "webs" of dementia are becoming stronger. It is harder to navigate through the day with connectivity. Thoughts are lost almost as quickly as they are lived. Joy of Goodwill "finds" in the morning will be forgotten by the afternoon. It breaks my heart. I have to try very hard to leave it all on the table—not feeling any sadness, as Moma will pick up on it and get upset that her illness is "burdening" me. She then tries to push me away, wanting to hire a personal caregiver rather than "hurt" me. It is such a hard position to be in for us both.

There comes a time when you must accept and find grace enough to move on. Find a path beyond the webs that tangle the mind and reach for the joy that remains. For surely, joy does remain, even if harder to recognize.

Moma's Reality

The process of dementia varies from person to person. Symptoms are similar, though not everyone experiences the same ones. To complicate things further, since your loved one with dementia is regressing, they will have memories from their own past. Possibly before you, the caregiver, were born. This makes everyone's symptoms different, as they are personal to them and new to you.

I read recently that in order to better love Moma with dementia, it is wise to embrace her reality rather than trying to bring her into mine. This is so very true. We can be talking about one thing and within the time frame of the conversation, the end of the subject is about something altogether different. I figure, her reality changed, and it is best for me to follow along with it. Think of it as a "condensed" conversation, so we can touch base on several things at once. It works.

Another time I experience this is when Moma talks about the fish in the pond out back. There is a pond and it does have fish... but the fact that she feeds these fish is her reality. She believes that by chopping up her leftovers and placing them down the kitchen drain, they are coming out in the pond. She even explains to me how she can see their mouths on the top eating her food. At first, I thought it best to keep her in "real" reality and explain to her that the water goes to the city sewer. She would agree, if only to shut me up, and then proceed to chop food for the next day. This time I said, "I bet they are hungry today."

I love being with Moma—even in her reality.

Part 16
Trusting

November 2015 – January 2016

Moma in Thailand, 1970.

News of the Day

The world is in turmoil. Not a day seems to go by without someone hurting someone else. We seem to be our own worst enemy. It's mind-boggling and painful.

My mom asked me the other day about the world news. How much do I say? She asks the adult questions yet interprets information like a child. She hears drips and drabs in her travels. If you answer too real, it could overwhelm her. If you answer too childlike, it could insult her. I find myself realizing that she won't remember what we are saying … but for the moment, it impacts her highly. I listen to her reactions, her tone. This helps guide me to my next word. Take a deep breath, ask God for guidance, and move forward. Trust that it will work out.

Allowances for God

I will be the first to admit that there have been times... more of late... that I question why. I get that Moma has dementia and feel that we have a bit of a handle on that.

But when issues arise because of it, I find myself asking God why. Isn't it enough that she has dementia? Does she really have to go through such pain and confusion? Why can't my "willing" it to be better help? Isn't that what prayer is for? God knows I do enough of that. I find myself even getting "angry" that she is put through so much. I feel that everything I do to protect her and keep her happy just sometimes doesn't seem good enough. Bottom line—I get angry with God.

Funny, the other day Moma and I were talking about something that was frustrating her, and she said the coolest thing. After complaining about whatever was bothering her, she calmly said, "I make allowances for God." Wow, what a fascinating statement. Made me think very deeply.

First off, I expect God to be in charge... of everything. Like a parent to a child, He just is. But if you think about it, how many times did our parents make a decision that we didn't like. At our "ripe old age of 15," did we ever disagree with their decision? It never dawned on us that there was a reason for their choice. Nor did we really care. As an adult, I find that the questioning of decision is still alive and well. Only now, I look to God. Poor Man isn't even here to defend Himself. Problems are laid before Him. Judgments are placed on Him. Anger is directed at Him. It's as if we need a higher person in charge to allow our problems to be placed upon.

God wants that from us, as we are His children. But I never thought of making allowances for Him. Truth is, we should, as we don't see the full picture as He does and therefore, we surely can't come to a judgment with only most, if not just some, of the facts. It's hard not to show our anger... and I am guessing at this time He's pretty used to it, with me at least. I always say *sorry* and *thank you* after the reasoning becomes clear to me. I try to say that I will be more accepting the next time, but He knows I will mess up again. It's all good, as while we are trying to make allowances for Him, I can promise you that He surely makes allowances for us.

Thank you, God.

The Eve of Past Extremes

Life will, on occasion, make choices for you, whether you want it to or not. You wake up one day and *bam*, a curveball you didn't see coming. It can take your breath away and leave you stunned. As I sit here on the eve of Moma's accident one year ago tomorrow, I am flooded with emotions from every angle. That fateful day brought about a life-altering event.

The pure trauma we went through was the initial effect, causing deep-rooted issues that touched Moma's dementia. This was overwhelming.

The physical pain of the accident lasted months, with the mental recovery remaining around still today. Moma never regained her confidence; that, along with her progressive dementia causing the need of a caregiver, has put a new spin on her life. We lost a bit more of her after the accident and the trauma of the recovery. She, for the most part, knows who I am but not who I was, forgetting personal things about me—about us.

We skipped the coin tradition altogether this New Year, as Moma couldn't retain what the big deal was in this day we called New Year's Eve. Our long-standing black-eyed peas on New Year's Day was passed over without even a thought. The day had no meaning or tradition at all. I cry for the loss of "us."

But what this year has also given us is the acceptance of Moma taking on a caregiver. This was such a blessing. Along with that, she allows me to call her every day without fail at 9 AM, and we take our morning pills "together." Miracle.

So as I sit and ponder, (one of Moma's new go-to words of late that I rarely heard her use before), I can genuinely say that God has been watching over and guiding us through this past year of extremes. After all the horrible—came the beauty of a safer life with more direction and protection overall.

Thank you, God.

Part 17
Slipping Through Time

March 2016 – June 2016

Moma in Virginia, 1976, age 46.

Moma's Birthday

March 10, 2016

Happy birthday to you. Happy birthday to you.
Happy birthday, dear Moma. Happy birthday to YOU.

My dear Moma, you are my best friend and angel. I say to you that, though there are times you may not remember this... I promise I will never forget.
    "We'll do this again next year, Moma."
    Atwaba—Sussy

"Present"

March 23, 2016

Fifteen minutes with Moma. That's what we shared this morning on our 9 AM call. We spoke with clarity and connected with personal emotion. It was pure joy. I know Moma is always "there," but today she was "present."

I will remember this morning forever.

Present, Past Time

Days turn into weeks and then slip into months. It's amazing how quickly time passes by without even a notice.

With Moma, days stand still in the moment, all the while her mind returning to her past. I find more now that her days blur together, as her past barrels forward. Once, "go out days" were fun outings to Goodwill and Walmart. Now, by the afternoon, she frequently will have forgotten her outing from that morning. I have Fafa take pictures of her newfound "goodies" and talk with her about them throughout the days, trying to keep her mind somewhat focused.

Contrarily, old memories will pop in and out all day long. Most are upsetting thoughts from her long-ago past—yet her dementia allows these memories to settle in as if they were new and current. I softly tell her these "current" memories are from her past and will not affect her now. She breathes a happy sigh, only then to feel mentally unstable for the confusion to have happened at all.

There is such injustice in dementia. You are expected to live in the present, while reliving the past—believing it to be now and having no possible idea of the future.

It steals your very life.

Mother's Day

What does Mother's Day mean to you? A pretty card, beautiful flowers, a special thank-you for being you?

All the above.

Today is Mother's Day and though I thanked Moma for being my special mom, she had no idea what the fuss was for. Moma's dementia has disconnected her from "reality." At least the reality in the traditional sense.

The most part of the day was treated as any other. I felt a sense of sadness that we weren't celebrating her and all her accomplishments. But then I realized, we were.

Our "reality" was that we were sharing that moment in time, together, laughing and living. There didn't need to be an understood reason why or any special celebration. Truth is, we should celebrate every day like it is special. The world would be a better place.

From now on, I will try to see each day as a "special day" and meet it with excitement. Every day, after all, is a journey—it could bring smiles or tears but a journey it is. And a journey shared is always a blessing.

"Let's do this again next year, Moma."

Four-Foot Teddy Bear

Speaking of journeys, dementia can bring some doozies. People helping themselves to dinner in Moma's kitchen, small fish swimming in her toilet bowl, little lizards playing "peekaboo" on her kitchen wall. But this one stands out to me:

Moma had found a four-foot teddy bear at Goodwill. She brought it home and was very proud of it. Luckily, Fafa had taken a picture of it for me earlier that day. It was late evening when Moma called me and said there was a "woman" who had helped herself into her home and sat down to watch TV with her. Moma sneaked into the kitchen to call me and whispered her concern that the woman wasn't leaving. How to proceed without upsetting Moma yet make her feel comfortable that she was not in danger.

I remembered the picture showed a bear sitting on the chaise lounge in the living room. Now to address her hallucination with tenderness.

I asked Moma if she could take the phone to the "woman" and let me ask her what her intentions were. She responded that she believed the woman spoke Spanish. I reminded her that I could manage with my "Spanglish" and asked her to try for me. She left to address the woman and returned explaining that "she" didn't respond to her.

I gently reminded her that she had found a very large bear today at Goodwill, and I think she might be sitting on the chaise lounge. I asked if that was where the "woman" was. "Why yes," Moma replied. We both had a belly laugh.

I explained to her that she probably fell asleep and had a daydream. The trick is to share with her a silly dream of mine every time she has one of her own. She worries that she is "losing it," to which I reply, "I lost mine already… if you find it, please let me know." She smiles.

My "Present"

Yesterday was my birthday. I had promised to always remind Moma of any special occasion, knowing she might forget, and so I did; I mentioned it in the morning.

Moma's response was an instant "Really?" as if she got it, but then the thought quickly slipped into a subject of no meaning. I won't lie—it saddens me that her thought process disconnects so easily from a conversation.

Throughout our days, Moma calls me her mother, sister, or neighbor. Today, I so badly wanted to be her daughter.

I moved on with my day and later that night the opportunity came up once again to mention my birthday. This time, though surprised yet again, she seemed to put the words to thought and actually said "happy birthday" to me. For a moment, she was present.

Present... that's funny. When people think of birthdays, they think of presents. For Moma and me, the best gift she could have ever given me was that moment of being "present."

Thank you, Moma and God, for that moment. "We will do it again next year, Moma."

Part 18
Life with Hard Edges

June 2016 – October 2016

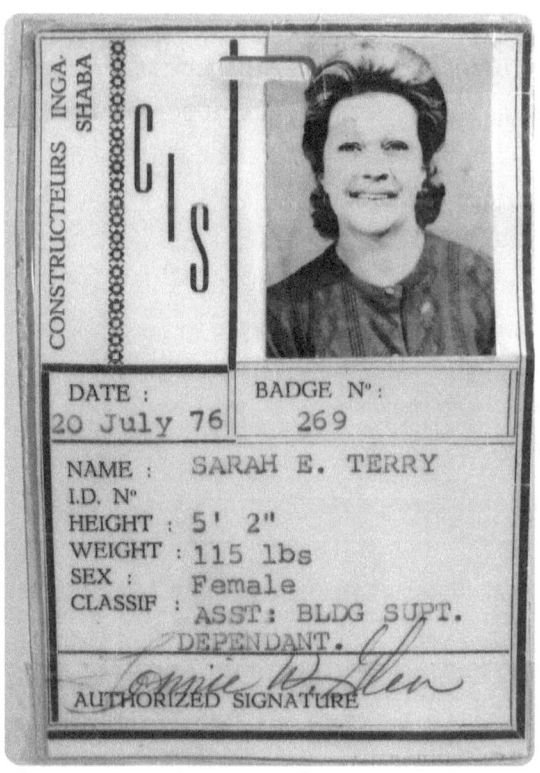

Moma's Zaire identification card in 1976.

Rerun

Moma is in the stage now where she has memories that "haunt" her. Sad that dementia robs you of your mind yet causes old memories to seem current. It causes today to seem like yesterday, making you feel out of control when you realize you are stuck in a rerun of your past. I said to her this morning to let the memory be, as she is worrying about something that God took care of years ago. Easier said than done when you can't distinguish between memory and reality.

We find ourselves making new memories throughout our lives. With dementia, these are fleeting and may be forgotten within the hour. How sad it is to be unable to create a new moment in your life.

I purchased a Lokai bracelet limited edition sponsoring Alzheimer's. I love the meaning behind it. The concept is beautiful... highs and lows of your life, while all other beads are your journey between. Such is life. It is wonderful to remember there will be highs even with the lows—you just have to keep the faith.

Two-Hand Rule

Moma and I were talking about life and how difficult it can be. Even with her dementia, there are times that, if you let her be, she carries on a very deep conversation.

She was talking about reaching for things. While you can reach out with either hand, we instinctually reach with the hand we gravitated to as a youngster. Some of us are considered right-handed while others are left. It's not something we practice as a child, but rather something we are inclined to. From that time onward, we are dominant in that hand. As adults, we are still using that found knowledge from childhood.

With dementia, I swear the bumps in the road just "appear" while you're in forward motion. You will find the two-hand rule applies often. While reaching out to catch the pieces with your dominant hand, be prepared to reach for safety with your other hand to keep from falling. Life with dementia is truly a balancing act.

Remember, "it's not how many times we fall that matters, but how many times we get back up." I love that saying.

Spiraling

There will be days, more often as you progress, that dementia takes over. It swoops in and whisks away what little of your loved one remains and leaves in their place a hyper, angry, hurting, and hurtful person.

The first time this happened to us, I lost it. I was scared and sad while taking everything personal. Who was this woman screaming into the phone, acting out like a child having a tantrum? Saying meaningless yet painful things—spiraling out of control.

It's like falling in a hole... the fall begins a downward decline that causes her mind to spin. Things pop in and become part of her "twister" that have nothing to do with the moment. Her mind becomes more and more obsessed with "stuff"—it becomes a nightmare for us both.

I must remain as calm as possible, otherwise she becomes enraged, both with my help and with the thought of putting me through this spiral. She has said often that she wants to get away from me, so I don't see her this way and she doesn't hurt me.

Sadly, it is at these times I grasp for her the hardest.

ID

Today, dementia took over. It started with a phone call from Moma saying she couldn't find her ID. I reminded her that we have a spare, but rather than this comforting her, she started her downward spiral of feeling "controlled" by me, since "I feel she can't be trusted." A common response when she feels out of control and things confuse her. Sadly, you must find a way to regain control without her feeling you are doing so, as being out of control to her means she can't live alone. It means she has become a "burden." Neither are correct, of course, but are very real to her.

On this day, I had Fafa lay out the spare ID so Moma could "find" it and all was well. If only all problems could be solved so easily.

God Is in the Driver's Seat

I had a meltdown the other morning with God. I will admit I even swore.

I called Moma to take her pills. Fafa has been in charge of filling them, which keeps me feeling safe. All Moma has to do is take the container from the drawer and count pills with me before taking them. We had taken her pills and were in the process of putting the container back in the drawer when suddenly, with the phone lying on her table, I heard Moma's count again. My heart sank. I yelled into the receiver, but nothing worked. She returned to the phone so proud. I panicked but kept it together so she wouldn't feel as if she had done something wrong—which would have caused more trauma.

Once off the phone, I felt such failure in protecting Moma. I immediately made calls to learn any consequence of this double dose. I was assured there would be no side effects, thank God. Of course, changes were made to her pill taking, and I was reminded, yet again, that God is in the driver's seat and keeps His promise.

The Love Word

I find that Moma's conversations are becoming much more repetitive. We discuss the same things daily. The words get placed differently in sequence, sometimes making little sense, but the plot is consistent.

She believes humidity in the house is causing her to dry her clothes repeatedly, she believes she lost her wine, she is always running out of pee pads even with new packages in the closet, Ila (her deceased sister) calls fusing at her daily, daddy is late coming home (he has been gone over twelve years) ... these are some of the frequent conversations we have every day.

I miss talking with her so much. It's hard for her to follow any conversation unless it is one of her usual ones. She always asks about "Big John" and loves talking on the phone with our dog Vinny. I find myself adding words in for her in my mind that I know she would want to be said. Like today is rabbit-rabbit day and was always shared first thing beginning of each month for good luck. This superstition's origin is unknown, though is found in Britain and North America as folklore with numerous variations practiced. Since it is meaningless to Moma at this point, I say it for us both. I think she would be happy about that. She does still say "I love you," which means the world to me. Days that she is hurtful, I say the love words for her. I know she would like that too.

"I love you, Moma."

"I love you more, Little Rene."

Moma's Tree Revisited

"There is a tree in front of Moma's home that has been there from the beginning. She used to plant impatiens around it. She watched it grow over the many years."

The previous paragraph is from the chapter titled Moma's Tree. Moma speaks of this tree almost daily. Her story of the tree changes as time goes on. It is now a tree that she planted not knowing she wasn't allowed to. She found it in the woods and watched it grow into the tall tree it is today. She laughs that it no longer offers shade, as the leaves are far above her window. She "remembers" planting it to hide the dumpster. I remind her now she has a front-row seat for anything tossed out by her neighbors that she might want to save. She smiles.

Tonight, we talked about her friendly tree and remarked that the top is reaching for Heaven while the trunk and roots are sturdy on Earth.

As we hope for in life, nature is our teacher.

Find the Words

I got a phone call from Moma. The time was 1:30 AM. My heart skipped a beat.

"Is your father alive?"

This question has become a daily inquiry. It is followed with—"How long has he been dead, I just spoke to him earlier today? He kissed me and said he had to go out for a while. Will he be back for dinner? How did he die?"

She goes through the same emotions each time. First, she wonders why she remembers him as if he is still here. When she remembers all the "bad" things from their lives, she wants him to stay "on his side of Heaven" when she gets there. I promise her God will see to it that all is happy in Heaven, so He will work it out for her. This seems to help the matter.

One can only hope to find the strength and some combination of words that help the dementia situation at that moment.

Usually it is safe to say the same words will be spoken. On some occasions though, you will find yourself "grasping" for the right word, any word. Find it, say it, and run with it. It seems to always work out somehow.

Moma's African Kolwezi ID card in 1976.

Part 19
Promise Me Always

October 2016 – March 2017

Moma with Dad in 1978.

Always

I sit here at my table overlooking our lake. It is serene, like a mirror reflecting the sky, with multiple colors of autumn leaves that are along the shoreline. Vibrant red, golden yellow, and the constant color of evergreens. I love every season, but there is something about autumn that is calming after the heat and noise of summer. A time to enjoy and reflect... and breathe.

Moma's dementia is progressing as normal. Sadly, she is aware of it, and that alarms her sometimes. I calmly remind her that she is still in charge of her daily life with cleaning, eating, and taking care of Nayla. This makes her happy. Meanwhile, I am blessed to have Fafa in control of medications, outings, and literally anything I ask for, including finding her remote control for watching her favorite show on Monday nights.

Overall, things are going well. That's not to say I don't have meltdowns. A few... okay, several, but things always work out.

Moma said the other day she "called" on God, only to feel her message went "straight to His voice mail. Busy I guess—but He promises to answer all in due time."

All I know for sure is I am still very blessed to have Moma with me. Good days, not so good days—as she would say, "That's life." One of her sayings of late is, "God gives you life. You have to live it."

We are living it together, Moma, "next door, next door."

After a tough day, Moma said something precious to me—"Promise me that if I lose me again, you will be there."

"I promise you always, Moma. *Always.*"

Her World

Our conversations are becoming smaller yet. By that I mean the topics are repetitive, as always, but of late, new thoughts or conversations get lost in "dementia translation." The other day I started to share my last chapter with Moma about our lives. When I began with the lake scene, she chimed in that she, too, faces a lake out back.

She went on to tell me all about her "lake and the many birds and fish" she and Nayla watch from her porch. I realized then that any words I might share with her couldn't mean as much as the thoughts of her own lake. It made me happy and sad at the same time.

Sad because we can't carry on any new conversation in her world. Happy because she is content to be there.

I am happy to visit her there.

Robert...Robert

"Is your father alive?"

Once again, this question visits us. She relives her 54 years of marriage so vividly that she gets mad at him when he is late for dinner. It is so real to Moma that I have found myself agreeing he would be right back... only to get caught in my own web when she ponders a moment and blurts out, "He's dead!"

He's been gone only 12 years, so overall, the married time certainly outweighs the time he has been gone. It is hard to calm her though, when she just "knows" he's in the house.

Recently, she was so spooked that he was in her condo that I held on the phone to have her go check. I listened sadly as she checked every room calling his name.

"Robert...Robert." My heart broke.

Once she was comfortable that he was not there, the confusion of why she must relive this came up.

"Why is God punishing me?" she cried out. All I could do was cry with her.

Never Let Go

Moma and I shared rabbit-rabbit this morning, and I explained to her that it was New Year's Day. The meaning is lost to Moma, so we skipped our usual coin-and-peas traditions in order to keep her from feeling how much she has lost. Moma told me I speak dementia... I guess I do.

So much to catch up on since my last writing. The past six weeks have been a whirlwind. Our beloved Fafa was accepted into nursing school, which made my world stop, though I am happy for her. She was kind enough to find and train a replacement and will still be available for drive-bys when not in school. The new caregiver seems very nice, and most important, Moma seems to like her.

With the new year, I pray our lives slow down and become more mundane. I pray for better health with continued guidance and strength to navigate the twists and turns of both our dementia and regular worlds.

I ask that God "never let go."

My Prayer to God

"I am grateful for God and all of His wonderful blessings and guidance.

"A special prayer to please continue to guide and protect us always.

"Please don't ever let go." Amen.

Memory Sign

Memories. Moma is constantly visited by them. Good ones, bad ones, sadly, all confusing ones. They all blend together into her world of today. I softly explain such things as Daddy being in Heaven again. She is silent while trying to pin that information somewhere in her brain for next time. She returns to being happy, if only for a short while.

But of course, memories return. Moma begs me to find something to make them stop. Something to make her feel "normal" again. I crumble silently. I explain to her that memories are very normal. They are what has made us who we are. They are the reason for gray hairs and laugh lines. They are us.

I suggested that Moma make a sign of memories to put on her fridge. Rather than fearing them, let it be a reminder they are part of us, our day. She then said something that was awesome. She said she would read the "memory sign" and choose which one to revisit at certain times.

Now her memories can be visited by her on her terms and she will smile.

What a wonderful idea.

Atwaba

I told Moma I love her this morning. She responded with, "You love me what…"

I then said, "I love you all the world and back again." She remembered and said the words with me. Glorious.

I'm Me

Dementia is an illness that just keeps on taking. Taking a little bit more of you each day. Your memories, your manners, your routines... the very person you were. Looking back at Moma's and my journey, I can revisit past chapters and see the decline through the years. It is disheartening and overwhelming to know tomorrow will come, only to learn yet another bit of who Moma was will be replaced with who she is now.

The only thing that can keep you strong through all of this is to realize she is still in there somewhere. Moma has become more challenging, having outbursts almost daily. They pass after a bit and later that night she will say what a great day she has had, only to possibly relive the trauma again tomorrow.

Memories and thoughts become intertwined to make an episode that never really happened but seems so real in Moma's mind. By comforting her with the reality that her concern didn't happen, her relief is then quickly disrupted by the fact her mind "made it up."

With all the madness of dementia, after calming down one night, Moma said the best thing... she said, if someone were to ask her who she is, she would say, "I'm me."

Moma's Birthday

March 10, 2017

Today is Moma's 87th birthday. I usually write "Happy Birthday" on her day, which I will before the end of the day but… I need to say something first.

In the years since learning of her dementia diagnosis, it seems a lifetime has passed. In a way, it has.

With each passing day, Moma ebbs and flows with emotions. Her demeanor changes, along with her whole personality. Verbal and action filters are blurred. Absolutely nothing she says or does surprises me anymore. She is living her life in reverse. Yet, as she said in the last chapter, she is "me."

I still reach her inner core. Maybe not as often as I'd like, but she is still there. Beneath the confusion, the anger, and frustration, she is still "me." Something she will say reminds me of "us." I live for moments like that.

Today started with Moma asking who I was. I have learned to let that roll off and keep going. It's not important that she knows who I am, but rather that she laughs on the phone with me regardless. It is a comfort to feel her love, whoever I am to her at that moment. There are still times that she finally remembers who I am, remembers "us"… and that is amazing.

Dear Moma—

*Happy birthday to you. Happy birthday to you.
Happy birthday, my dear Moma. Happy birthday to you—*

Boop-boop.
"We will do this again next year, Moma." I love you.
Atwaba—Sussy

—"Little" Rene

Part 20
Balancing on Stepping-Stones

May 2017 – July 2017

Moma with her yellow ribbon, in 1979.

Navigating Through Thorns

Two months have passed since Moma's birthday. A few days after her day, she fell and bumped her side. There were no signs of anything serious on her body, thank God, but she was stiff. Her doctor advised Tylenol and rest.

One morning, her caregiver arrived and tried to let herself in. Moma was in such a sound sleep, not even me calling both phones woke her. She had the inside chain on the door as added security, which she always did at night. Sadly, her neighbors became involved and broke the lock with a hammer. Once inside, they found Moma terrorized by the "break-in," shaking in bed, thinking something horrible was happening. I had her caregiver assess her and called her primary for a walk-in appointment. The neighbors called 911 instead.

One might think that was a good idea, but skip back two years ago in the hospital. It was just as hard on Moma this time, if not worse, as her dementia is further along. Initially they said she had a fracture in her hip and kept her overnight, while setting up rehab yet again. While preparing for another trip down to Florida, the hospital called and said the fracture they saw was the old one, and there would be no need for rehab. They would keep her one more night for pain management, and she would be released. This itself was wonderful news.

However, more was to come.

Beginning New Routines

Moma's dementia was alive and well after the hospital stay. She was quite irate while there and though happy to be home, seemed a bit removed and agitated with everything and everyone, especially me. In her mind, it was my fault she was put in the hospital. Of course, I understood but didn't quite know how to address it, as she was adamant to have nothing to do with me. How to orchestrate Moma's recovery and be anonymous?

For starters, I had her caregiver remove the latch from the front door. Moma was NOT happy, but I explained I had no choice, as it was per "orders of her doctor." Poor man, I blame him for a lot. This will allow easier access into her home and prevent, at least, this drama from happening again. She did, however, begin blocking the door with her walker at night.

Next, I used this incident as a way to implement Moma's pills to be given to her every day. I said that her doctor was required by her medical insurance to have a nurse give them to her from now on—in order for her to remain in her home. I added that she needed a half a pill every evening, per her doctor, which meant I had her caregiver there every morning and evening. Of course, with pills came eating just enough to make the pills work. Pills, breakfast, and dinner now covered. What a blessing!

You guessed it. I used this incident for everything I could, explaining I was being directed by all concerned to add the extra visits and all changes being made. Moma was mad at me already, so this seemed the opportune time to slip in more care. Did she fight me? Of course. Was it worth it? You bet!

With time, Moma began to settle into her new routine a bit better. It has been two months, and we still have some "pushbacks" from her, but they are becoming less each day. I opted to stay in Boston during this confusing time, for my appearance was the last thing she needed to be added into her newfound routine, especially with her frustration toward me currently. I am just so happy that I can help make her life safer and better.

I am just now beginning to exhale. Breathing is good. Thank you, God.

Candlelight

In my window I have a "Christmas" candle that I use every night. I love the old idea of leaving a candle in one's window, which dates back to Colonial days.

> *"There is not enough darkness in all the world to put out the light of even one small candle."*
> —Robert Alden

I leave our candle on every evening. It makes me feel uplifted. On gray, cloudy days, I put it on as a sign of trust that the sun will find its way out. I told Moma that it was my way of "reminding God" it is daytime :-)

Whatever your reason to reach for a bit of "light" in your day, do it, as life is hard. Remember that shadows are proof there is light nearby. Look for the light, or make it yourself, and smile.

Memory Connection

My birthday came and went without fanfare this year. Moma knows I'm familiar to her, but on many occasions, she doesn't know I am her daughter. When she does, she remembers nothing about me, but only this moment. She does, however, remember my husband, "Big John." Always makes me smile.

Many times, we visit old memories. I reach into my memory bank and try to draw a verbal picture for Moma. I love when I hear her say, "I remember that!" It makes all effort worth it. One time she said that I am her connection to her memory. True.

I knew this day would come. It has been arriving slowly each year. Only now it seems to be daily. I won't lie—it's sad, and I miss so much who she was and what we had. I hold onto the reality that she is still with me, only the mother/daughter relationship has shifted completely at this point. I can say that she has been and still is the best mom in the whole world. Only now, I have proof of her loving ways being instilled in me as I give them back to her.

Moma, I will always be the path to your memories, while we build new ones together every day.

Remember to Remember

"Drop dead. No, don't die. I want you to feel pain."

And so my day goes today. Moma is angry that she can't take care of herself. She is pushing back and rejecting care. Her mind is confused regarding her condition requiring a caregiver altogether. Angry, hateful words, so unlike the Moma that I know from before. This is the Moma of "the moment."

With dementia, they switch their moods on a dime. Remember to "remember" who your loved one "was" and still is, somewhere inside of this new tangled mind. Moma will come out of this and not even remember what she said. She will feel the aftermath of uneasiness from the outburst of her emotions. I will tell her that she has had a wonderful day, and all will be well.

At the close of a call tonight, I said to Moma, "I love you." Her response, with pride, was, "I love you because I can."

For that moment in time, I felt as if she knew who I was. That she could remember. It touched my heart and made me sob with sadness and joy.

Moma shopping.

Part 21
Flowers Still Bloom, Birds Still Sing

July 2017 – September 2017

Moma with Puchai in 1979.

Pure Magic

Tomorrow is John's birthday. I praise the day he was born and can't imagine my life without him. We have weathered so much through our years together and find ourselves holding onto each other for strength even now. I can tell you that Moma, no matter how far away her mind is, loves John. All I ever have to say is that I am the one married to "Big John," and she lights up. He gets on the phone and takes her to a place that is clear in her otherwise muddled thoughts.

"I love Big John." And so begins a conversation about our lives together, thus getting her off thoughts of dementia. It's magic.

Pure magic.

Angel Prayers

"Stop remembering that you forgot."

I find that Moma gets very upset when she realizes she has forgotten something. Trouble is, that while trying to figure it out, her thought process slides into another subject and she shifts to yet another matter. With this, she is in a never-ending cycle of confusion. I said to her the other day, "Remember what you have to and forget the rest." I wish it worked like that, for her sake. Always being in a state of uncertainty is awful for her.

Yesterday she said to me that she called on her angel a lot that day. She then added, "I wonder what they say when we hang up? Next…"

Kinda funny, if you think of it, as with the number of prayers they listen to, they probably do.

Joining in Heaven

Moma asks me almost every day if Daddy is still alive. As always, we talk it through and get to a "temporary" close of the conversation. We revisit how many years ago he died, how old he was, and the cause of his passing.

Today she surprised me with her clarity by figuring his age at passing and the number of years he's been gone to calculate what his real age would be today. She then said in panic, "What if he dies before I join him in Heaven?"

I assured her he wouldn't—then I cried.

48

Today I just turned forty eight,
I've been around awhile,
I've had my pleasures, up's and downs,
And covered many mile.
But in the year of forty eight
You came in to my life,
You made my days and nights fly fast
When you became my wife.
Before this dear my life was gloom.
I had no where to run,
You said "I DO" Became my wife
My clouds turned in to SUN.
And now with you beside me dear
With all your trust and faith,
Don't ever FRET, I'll be around,
For many years to come.

  I Love you
   your husband
     Bob

       DANANG, Vietnam
       JAN 27, 1967

Daddy's poem to Moma in 1967.

Dream

August 16, 2017. Dementia crept into my dreams for the first time last night. It has been many years since Moma was diagnosed, but I always had the space of dreams to share what we were before it stole her away from me. Last night she had dementia in my dream.

I was angry, then cried—then put one foot before the other and moved forward.

Remember the Flowers and Birds

It's raining today. Rain can be seen as gloomy and sad. It prevents you from doing some things as planned and can get your spirits down.

On rainy days, it is important to remember anything good associated with rain. The flowers and birds are happy. It washes away pollen and dirt. It makes things smell clean. It gives us an excuse to stay on the sofa and drink hot chocolate while watching reruns.

Life is partly how we choose to view it. There is little we can do about what life does to us, only how we accept it. We are responsible for our choices made, to push through and beyond life's issues.

Of course, with all that said, I got so mad at dementia the other day that I slapped my hand on the kitchen counter. Ask me how that went.

Life is hard. Be kind to yourself for being human. Find ways through the rain and even look for good things along the way. After the storm, flowers still bloom and birds still sing.

A Year Ago, a Year from Now

There comes a time in your life where you feel, actually know, that things are not in your control. Planning is a must in life, lest you are merely hoping things will fall into place with no energy needed from you. Sadly, plans quite often get redirected by "life," and the path you had laid out so clearly becomes covered with doubt.

I have learned over these past dementia years the feeling of defeat. It's a horrible emotion of brokenness that leaves you both wondering about your direction and wandering for a safe place to rest. It takes all you have to breathe in and out.

I can say no words to ease the heavy load. Only a quick fallback to something Moma always said to me before: "A year ago, a year from now."

This was meant to remind us that no matter how bad our moment is, think back a year ago to a problem that seemed so large and now may not be remembered at all, as time has softened it. Let's take a moment to look forward to a year from now. Will this current moment matter or also be faded by time? I have used this saying throughout so much of my life. I am using it now.

Breathe and reach for John.

Part 22
Self-Journey

September 2017 – February 2018

Moma with our dog at our home in Colombia, 1985.

Your Self-Journey

Being a caregiver is so much more than taking care of a loved one. It is also a journey into one's self. It makes you see your weaknesses and helps you find your strengths. It forces you to accept the most hurtful words and not allow them to reach your center core. It challenges you to find new ways of communicating—be it with words or merely actions. It makes you see things... differently.

Moma with newborn Nayla, 2005, age 75.

51–49

I have been living by these numbers for a while now: 51–49. Being a caregiver is never easy, but if you feel yourself falling in over your head, I find that by reminding myself of 51–49, it becomes a bit easier.

Emotions have lives of their own. We can't always control our feelings, though by reminding myself to be 51 percent caregiver to Moma and 49 percent daughter, it allows me to remain more rational. It helps hurtful words to be received as not personal. It makes me a stronger person to navigate the many ebbs and flows of dementia. This, in turn, helps Moma feel that her drama of the moment has my full attention, with the logic of her caregiver and the love of her daughter.

I will remember 51–49. It has become our mantra.

Revolving Door

Reflecting on our dementia journey—we have traveled so far in these eight years. I remember the feeling of being overwhelmed when her doctor told me over the phone her diagnosis of dementia. I was at work and in that instant, our world changed.

Every dementia journey is personal as your loved one regresses back in time, their own past. Now is when you find yourself trying to remember all the stories shared with you about their lives. Ironically, you will be sharing the memories back with them.

Find your "center" and recharge often. By staying grounded, you can slide in and out of their dementia reality with more ease. It becomes somewhat like a revolving door. While our loved one is living in their dementia world, you will have one foot in their world and one in yours. Be kind to yourself and step carefully.

You will be okay.

Shared History

While speaking to Moma this morning, she asked me what her life was about. Why is she still "here?" I reminded her who she is and what she means to me but then added a tangible reason too.

I explained that, though I have been with John for thirty years, she is my go-to source to know everything prior about my life. I said that speaking with her is like looking at a scrapbook of our life's events. Times we have shared, memories. As we reach back into our lives, she will sometimes remember in excitement. It's like finding a puzzle piece.

You can only pray to find all the pieces before they are lost to time. What a sad disease.

God's Dance

Why, God, do you challenge me so—do I not show my love?
Is my devotion not seen?
While I manage and question all things in between.

Could it be that I've yet learned how to let go?
And listen more closely for answers that flow yet, drift far away...
So very far—
that I miss the fact they are here in my life to be read like a map.

Help me to balance
and awaken my trust.

Trust in Your timing of all things, I must.
All things divine and in Your own time—
Teach me the dance of Yours and of mine.

Amen.

30-Minute Visit with God

I know we are taught to accept God's will and know He holds the master plan. Overall, I do follow this rule of thought—but there are times harder than others to find peace. Moma would ask many questions of me. I tried very hard to answer each one as many times as needed. There came some questions that I would say to her, "That's a God question—write it down on your list, Moma."

It is during these times that I ask God to please allow me, upon arrival in His great presence, to have thirty minutes of His wisdom for clarification. I promise that all of my questions will fit into this timeframe as I know He is very busy. At times of frustration, I add the issue to my list. It's funny, over the years, how the questions change. What resolves itself, what isn't important today or what has become clearer.

All in His time.

Snapshot of Us

You will find that, in caring for your loved one, you will change within yourself. While the "ride" is always worth it, there will be times that you find yourself losing your balance. This is an abridged version to this point of Moma's and my journey.

It has been eight years since I learned of Moma's dementia, though she was tested and diagnosed almost a year before they told me. Moma wanted to keep it quiet. I went through an array of emotions, as you read in chapter one, to finally get to acceptance. I read and studied anything I could on the matter, as it gave me some grounding, though be aware that each case is very different. You will find, the more you learn, the less you seem to know. Be strong, as the knowledge is still necessary for you to accept your loved one's actions and find some solid ground to stand on.

I promise you—that ground will be shaken daily. I have found caregiving to be ever changing. Moma has already gone through so many stages, and I must keep up or fall. You will be faced with someone who looks like your loved one but acts totally different. This is so hard as you expect to be with the loving person you know yet will often get the child with no filters and hateful words. You will need to place such times in a neutral part of your day and know it will pass. Though you might still feel the sting of the words and actions, they will be lost soon and replaced with laughter. This, too, will take a toll on you, and you must manage it in your own way (mine has been writing), or you will become overly depressed.

I am saddened every day for the loss of who "we were," yet try to find some joy for the love we still share. Sometimes Moma doesn't know me—but we still manage to be two people on the phone finding something to smile about. I pretend to be whoever she thinks I am. I refuse to let dementia steal everything from us. Refuse.

You will find that uncertainty will try to get the best of you. There is always a nerve in the pit of my stomach, not knowing what will happen on the next phone call. This part has caused anxiety for me. You know you need to be somewhat in control of things, yet you have never felt so out of control in your life. It's scary, I won't lie.

I now read, along with dementia books, stress management and books on loss of loved ones. Though Moma is still here with me, thank God, there is such a large part of who she was that has already been lost to dementia, and even more I lose daily. You must never forget to care for yourself while caring for your loved one, or you, too, can get lost. Find someone to hold onto. Mine is John.

Love and strength to us all.

I Received a Call

I received a call this morning.
She said, "And who are you?"
I very quickly realized she didn't have a clue.

We spoke of fears and anger, threw in frustration, too.
It seemed to last for hours but for a time or two...
I seemed to reach her "center." Her thought became more clear.

Her memory was forming but not sure from which year.
Memories flow boundlessly.
Yesterday becomes today, thus creating delusions of life along the way.

Life that has become a panic every day,
seldom recognizing things or knowing what to say.

But every once in a while, she takes a pause to see,
the one that she is speaking to is actually—me.

Dementia is a demon. It takes loved ones away,
but deep down in our hearts, our love will always stay.

I love you, Moma,
Atwaba.

Part 23
Puzzle Pieces on the Floor

March 2018 – May 2018

Moma with John, 1988, age 58.

Moma's Birthday

March 10, 2018

Happy birthday, dear Moma.
May your day be filled with good thoughts and memories.
Leave the bad ones for another day.
I pray for you that you stay above dementia—if I could be so bold, for the whole day.
May you laugh and enjoy today.
May you find peace and comfort in what you do.
May you be ... you.
I love you,

Little Rene

I am so happy to say that Moma did have a very good day. Though dementia was obviously present, it didn't take over, and Moma laughed and found joy on her day. I can't think of a better gift than to have the privilege of being yourself. Thank you, God.

Happy birthday to you. Happy birthday to you.
Happy birthday, dear Moma. Happy birthday to you.

Boop—boop.
I love you, Moma, Atwaba.
We will do this again next year.

Emotions and Actions

I find writing about Moma's and my "dance" to be therapeutic. It is my way to channel the words and emotions of our day. I would like to say there are more happy times than sad, but of late, not true. Being Moma's sounding board is needed by her, as she would have no one to share her fears and frustrations with if not for a caregiver. If not for me.

One would think that putting such sad times on paper would be counterproductive. I find, instead, that once I place them on paper, they become words, merely letters on a page, that cannot hurt and can be rationalized in the scope of things.

Moma had an outburst this morning and called me a bitch. She then hung up on me. By the next call, she asked if we were still friends. Always, Moma, always.

Don't let their emotions direct your actions.

Breathe, smile, and go on.

Puzzle

"Good morning, Moma, how are you today?" "Oh good...you know me?"

And goes so many of our calls of late. Not to say the conversation doesn't get better, as it usually does, but it seems more and more that I need to remind Moma not just who I am, but rather who she is. We touch base on any corner of her life that comes to mind. Like a puzzle, we are putting pieces of herself together to create a memory. Of course, the pieces are fresh out of the box each time and need to be turned upright and put into groups. We start with the corners and fill in the edges. Then comes the challenge of the "picture" itself.

Sadly, it seems the pieces get mixed daily—now and again getting lost on the floor. Recover as many as you can find and move forward.

Conversation with Daddy

May 15, 2018

Fourteen years ago this morning, Daddy went to Heaven. I visited with him today and shared all that has happened since he left. I promised him I am taking care of Moma and always will.

Moma's dementia has progressed to the point that she isn't aware of much anymore. Our conversations are about whatever pops in her mind at the time. Laundry, her cat, the woman that sits in the tree outside her window holding a cat. She is now experiencing non-scary delusions. She is not afraid but is also not in touch with reality at all. She needs more overseeing. This makes my life calmer, as I know she isn't alone, but then again, she fights anyone doing anything in her home, causing outbursts daily. It is no longer enough to coordinate and manage affairs. I now find myself needing to manage Moma. This is a whole different stage of her dementia.

The talk of dementia care units has been brought up by her doctor. Such a scary thought. For over eight years I have been able to keep her safe and happy in her own home. Now she frequently doesn't recognize her surroundings and seems scared. My heart aches more each day. It has been an honor to do for Moma and coordinate her life, while sharing her dance. Now comes the hard part of making difficult decisions about her life.

Is anyone ever ready for this? I'm not.

Daddy, please ask God for guidance and direction. We need all the help we can get.

Daddy and me.

Part 24
Our New Journey Begins

May 2018 – November 2018

Moma on her way to Boston in 2018.

New Reality

"It is then that I carried you." The words from "Footprints in the Sand" poem. I have recited these words sooooooooo many times, holding onto the fact that God is with me, even when I feel lost and alone. I have never understood these words more than now.

Two weeks have passed since my last writing. I just reread the last chapter. I can still feel the desperate emotion in every word. The plea to my father to speak to God. My whole self feeling lost and broken.

May 29th, Moma started with 24-hour care in her home. I knew it was coming and probably should have started before it did, but I was blinded to think that all my efforts were enough to honor her wishes. However, there comes a time when the caregiver must make that hard decision and choice. Social workers would check on her and had cleared her all times before to live alone, with the coverage I kept adding. Not this time.

Not now. They said 24-hour care in her home or nursing home. My heart stopped.

I had noticed changes—more confusion, difficulty hanging up a phone after a conversation, agitation coming more often. The signs were there. I felt like a failure. All I have done to honor and keep her safe was no longer enough. I now must do the hardest, most loving job for Moma thus far.

24-Hour Care

Now came the reality of making it happen. Now. Right now, or the social worker said she would take her into custody there until I could arrange things. God had His plan ready, and I was able to start her 24-hour care immediately, with the help of her caregiver calling in on her friend to make up two 12-hour shifts.

Moma found this a huge invasion of privacy and fought every breath of the way. Her agitation was turned up 100 percent. She became physically combative, demanding the caregivers leave her home at once. Her home was the last thing she had left where she could pretend to be normal. This, too, has now been lost. Though I feel comfort in knowing she is safe at all times, the reality is that I must find another way to help her, as she feels like a caged animal.

I am losing my mind. Wait, I can't.

Smooth as Peanut Butter

I have so very much to share. Almost two months have passed since my last writing. Let's begin at the beginning…

Moma was under 24-hour care for three weeks. It was so very hard for her to handle. Thank God for her wonderful caregivers. It became apparent that keeping her in her home wasn't a long-time plan. We offered to take her out daily, even for walks, but she refused and became a recluse. It was not healthy.

We had begun efforts a while back to search for assistance here in Boston for her and Nayla—come that "possible" day. That day is now.

We found a wonderful nursing home just ten minutes away from us. It is part of a shrine that I have been going to for comfort over the years. We were able to manage a private room, which was very important, what with Moma losing her independence.

Knowing that she wouldn't recognize me, I coordinated with her doctor and her caregivers to fly her and Nayla here, without any incident, thank God. I still can't believe we managed it, but I know it was God's work.

I had been preparing her room for a week before she arrived. Personal touches, sunflowers, pictures, pillows. When we placed her in that night, it went "smooth as peanut butter," as Moma would say. A miracle.

The night she arrived was my 60th birthday. Funny, years of late, my day has come and gone with no fanfare. For this milestone birthday, I got the best gift of all, my Moma and Nayla.

New Surroundings

The next morning, I saw her face. She was so very tired last night, and today seemed rested. I had a rush of emotions, one of complete comfort having her so close and protected in a surrounding that would stimulate her, and one of complete fear of the unknown as to her reaction overall to her new surroundings.

She seemed happy to see me, and I felt she recognized my face a bit. She even appeared a bit happy to be here. Of course, the questions came as to when I would be "taking her home." She thought this was a daycare for her. I explained softly that her doctor was required to have her with someone 24 hours a day and felt this was a safer surrounding for her. She asked about Nayla, and I explained she was staying with us while she was here. It seemed to touch the surface of her mind, for the moment.

Dinnertime

It has been almost two months having Moma and Nayla here. I sit in awe that so much is behind us now. After all the years of pondering over the direction life would take us and how we would manage it, one day you wake up and it's done. You begin the recovery of all your panic attacks and sleepless nights. Though there are still issues ahead, the big move is behind us. Thank God.

Moma is beginning to fit in with her new "home." The trick is to make her world much smaller, with less confusion. I visit her daily and have learned that meeting up for dinner seems to work best. It is structured—I arrive a bit early to prep the room for "room service," we enjoy having her dinner together, and talk about her activities of the day and how well Nayla is doing with us. So well, in fact, that she has stolen my heart. More on her later. We then have her buttermilk, which I bring daily, to her delight.

Afterwards, we put away her "laundry," which I take home to do, as it gives us a mission of hanging clothes; something she did all the time back home. Then the making of her bed, to get her familiar with her room and surroundings, and watching a bit of TV. Normal routine things. I find even though all these things can be done by the nursing home, when Moma and I do them together, it gives her a schedule and she feels involved—somehow still in charge. The eyelids become heavy and ready for a snooze.

We share "I love you" and hugs, I leave her room door ajar, tell her I will "lock the outside door" for her, then off I go, to return tomorrow. It works, thank God.

Teeth, Anyone?

Not to say that it is all easy. Moma is doing well but does have her bad times. And may I say, they are doozies.

Taking off her clothes and screaming angrily up and down the hall probably takes top billing. We have adjusted her medications to help keep her calm. I must remember she brought her dementia here with her and the outbursts come with it. Only now, she is in a controlled atmosphere, where I know she is safe.

Four months have passed, and her eating habits are changing. She has never been a big eater and has always been thin. I make sure to "supplement" her intake with goodies from home. This works, some of the time. Little things become challenging. She has taken her teeth out after eating breakfast and lunch to rinse them ... in someone else's room. Walking right by her own sink, thinking she is in her kitchen while eating, she wanders to her "bathroom" and cleans them, not realizing it is someone else's room. We also found them quite a few times downstairs in the kitchen, as she would take them out and leave them on her tray to clean later. I now have the nurses take them after eating, for safe keeping, returning them for every meal.

New Life

Moma has been interacting with the other patients, which is fantastic. The home has activities: having them decorate cupcakes and cookies; they do their nails in pretty pink; during the summer months, they take them to the garden and have them outside playing with the plants. It is a wonderful nursing home with wonderful people. The atmosphere and activities are good for her indeed.

I have been able to find warm clothing for her, even in the heat of the summer, at Goodwill shops. She has been cold these past few years and seems to enjoy getting "new things." I wish she was well enough to want to go out with me. Take her to see the beach, go to Walmart, John and I wanted to take her out for drives. I soon realized she finds no interest in leaving her "home." I am pleased in one way, as I know she is content and not having the urge to wander. It also means that her better years were spent in her own home with Nayla, which makes me happy that she had that irreplaceable time.

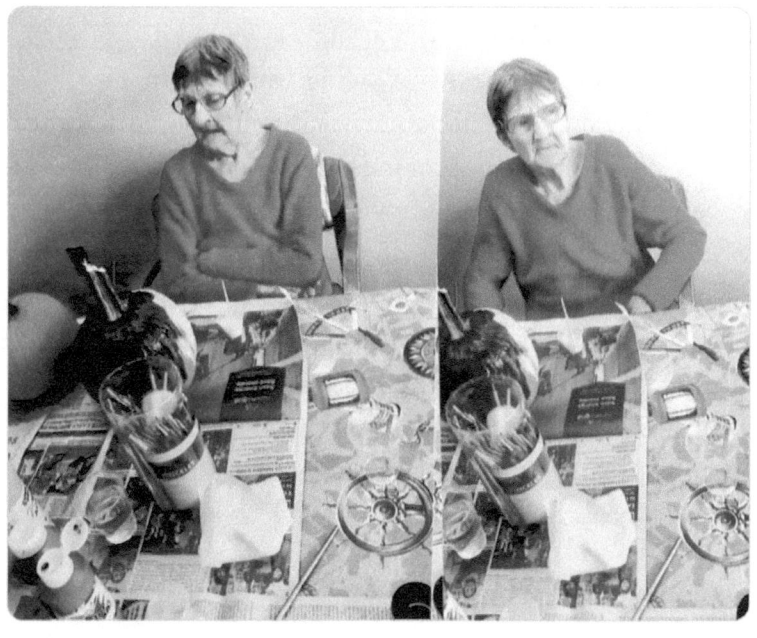

Moma is not too impressed by the nursing home's activity of painting pumpkins for Halloween.

Our Angel, Nayla

I want to talk about Nayla. Bringing her home was so scary, what with the two dogs and six birds. I placed a screen in the doorway of the bird room, which took care of them.

Rocky, my oldest dog, didn't seem to care much about Nayla at all. Vinny, however, was curious and is blind. This caused me concern that Nayla would swat at him. We used doggy gates for the introduction and began allowing time together with stern voices of "play nice" and long prayers. I will tell you that they all get along great now. It amazes me how she fits in to our crazy zoo after coming from such a solitary lifestyle.

God's work yet again.

Now to share the pure connection I have with this cat. Nayla has become my spirit animal. It's as if we communicate on a different level. I love all my animals, be assured. But with Nayla, it's different. The fact she shared 13 years of her life with my mom, time that I was so grateful Moma wasn't alone, makes her special. She was Moma's first caregiver. I owe her so much.

I've never had a cat for any length of time. In my early years, I was tested to be allergic to both cats and dogs. Cats, more so. I went to be tested last week and learned I am indeed still allergic to my dogs, but not cats? God's work again.

I find everything Nayla does fascinating. Okay, maybe not pooping where she shouldn't, and how on earth does it smell

THAT bad? Of course, my very first furball vomit, and the fact cats sometimes throw up just because they can... lots to learn.

All that said, the love and connection I feel for this one animal is overwhelming. I find myself watching her, wanting to be inside her mind to learn more about her and Moma. She is part tabby and part long-hair black from her mother. She looks magical and acts the same. I thank God that she is liking it here. He understood Himself all along.

Let go, let God.

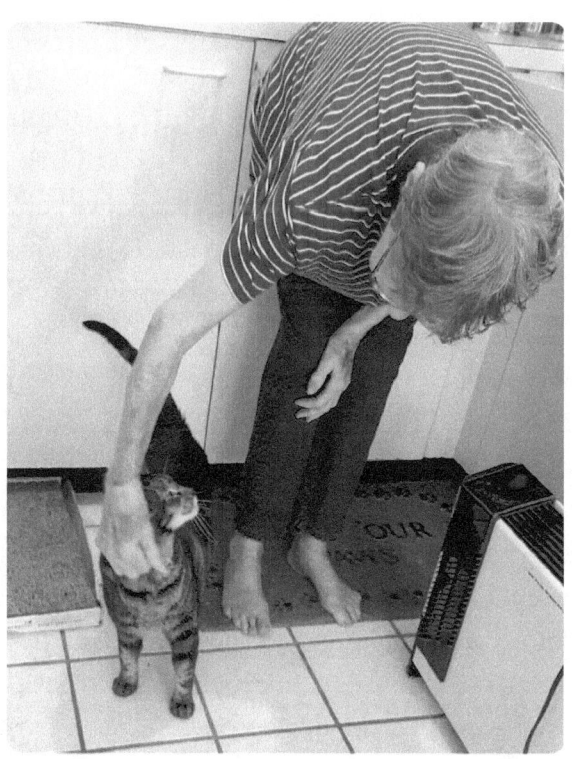

Intuition

The human mind is such a mystery. This chapter is to that point.

Moma was having outbursts one day at the home. She became very agitated, which was made worse by the surrounding nurses, in her opinion, not addressing her feelings. She had come out of her room and made a point that the man opposite her in the hall was in pain. He was one of her first friends when she arrived in June. It was now October. He had experienced a stroke and spoke very little. He communicated instead with gestures and emotions. The man in question was asked if he needed anything and if, indeed, was in pain. He responded no.

Moma continued to make an issue of their lack of attention to him. She repeatedly said that he was having trouble breathing. She became angry and combative, trying her best to assist the man. Finally, after administering her medication that was due, she calmed down and went to bed, exhausted.

The head nurse and I tried to determine where the anger was coming from. I was thinking that she was feeling her own pain and was acting it out through another person to get their attention. She had stumbled the day before—it made sense that she was feeling discomfort.

A few days went by. To everyone's surprise, the man in question began having trouble breathing. They determined he had bronchitis and was put on medication and a nebulizer.

Yet more time goes by, and I noticed that he was missing from his usual chair by the elevator. I asked about him and was told that he had been transferred to the hospital for his breathing. How sad he wasn't getting better. I called and wished him well in his recovery.

I didn't see him for two more weeks. When he did return, it was with the knowledge that he had end-stage lung cancer. The doctors advised the family he had three months to a year. My heart broke for him and his family. He was 70.

There are no good words about the outcome of this chapter. Only the realization of a demented mind, seemingly seeing in another human being something that no one, including trained nurses, could see with the naked eye. I'm not saying Moma knew about his cancer, only suggesting that she sensed his illness. Makes you think.

One day, he motioned to me he only had three left. I asked, "Months?" His reply was, "Weeks." He passed November 8, in the night—within three weeks of his return. He somehow knew and is now in a better place. Godspeed.

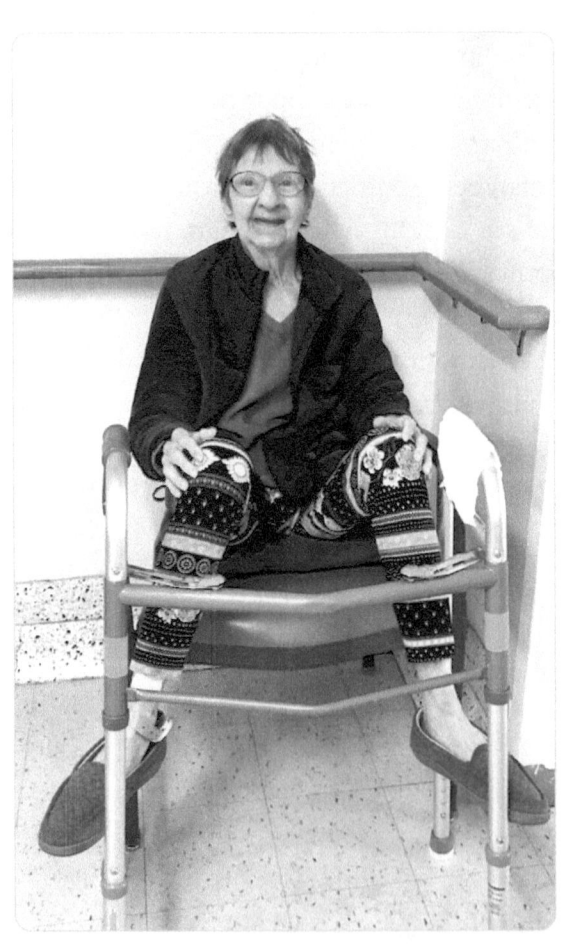

Moma sitting in her chair, using her walker as a footrest, in Boston, 2018, age 88. She loved putting her feet up when the floor was cold.

Part 25
Life Moving On

November 2018 – January 2019

Moma in Boston, 2018.

Closer to Heaven

There have been so many instances since bringing Moma to Boston that I have felt her angel smiling or Daddy giving us a big thumbs-up! This journey did, after all, seem to begin with a prayer on Daddy's anniversary of May 15 to have him ask God for guidance.

Right after getting Moma settled in, I was driving to visit her, and "Stardust" was playing on the radio. That is Moma and Dad's song. I will admit I listen to an oldies station—but that song RARELY plays. I heard it several times during the first month of her arrival.

When Moma lived at home, the tree she "planted" outside her kitchen window grew very tall. She would always say to me that all she could see was tree trunk, unless stepping outside. I would reply that the tree roots were planted firmly in the ground, while the limbs were reaching to Heaven.

Now Moma is on the third floor of the nursing home and has a wonderful view of Boston Harbor overseeing the outskirts of the airport, where I spent 25 years working. The night view is filled with lights. She faces the shrine with the Madonna that was shipped over from Italy years ago. It lights up at night. Her view is a very peaceful and beautiful one. She can see the treetops swaying in the wind. Makes me smile, as she finally gets to see the top of "her" tree. She, too, is closer to Heaven.

Settling In

I'm not saying things haven't been hard, but overall, I couldn't have written it much better. Moma is quite comfortable with her room. Her favorite thing is her bed and her pillow, which I bought from Walmart. She rearranges things in her room to make her feel like she is doing housework. I have made sure that everything in her room is "dementia proof" and can't break or cause her harm.

I have told her all the other residents are her new neighbors. She always feels comforted by the fact the nurses are there 24 hours a day. She has been participating in activities from time to time, which makes me thrilled.

I thank God for all our blessings.

Feeling of Happiness

This will be the first Thanksgiving and Christmas Moma and I have shared in thirty years, on the actual day.

Traveling home, as I did during my Delta days, you would never find a standby seat on any holiday. I would always travel on alternate days and claim that time as our holiday.

Moma hasn't been aware of "special days" for a very long time now. All days flow together for her. Daily, I ask how her day has been, to which she replies, "I have had a good day doing laundry, housework, and gardening." She never remembers any activities she might have participated in that day, but she does "feel" the contentment they bring to her. The girls in charge of activities take pictures of her for me, which are priceless. I keep them on her closet door, along with all her pictures of family from her condo. We visit them often to jar her memory.

With dementia, it's all about the feeling you experience rather than the experience itself. Seeing Moma getting involved with her surroundings is wonderful. She seems happy, thank God.

Know You Will Be Okay

I sit and "ponder" today watching the rain wash away the snow and ice left from a storm a few days ago. Funny how things can be "washed" away with a little rain. I watch as the leaves on a large oak tree dance and whistle in the wind. They remain until springtime. Most trees shed their leaves in fall—but not all. It's like God keeps some around for our entertainment. The sound is very soothing.

While our lives are spinning at a blurred pace, find something in nature that slows your mind and allows you to remember that all things are a cycle. All moments pass and flow into another.

Breathe, focus, know that you will be okay. January 24, 2019.

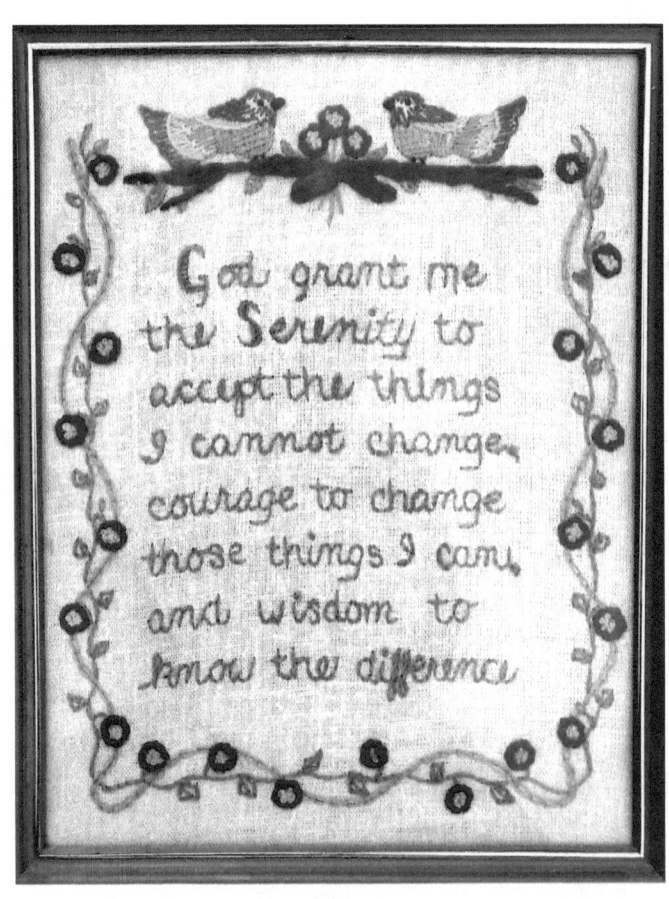

One of Moma's needlepoint creations.

Part 26
Homeward Bound

March 11, 2019

Moma in assisted-living in East Boston, 2018.

God Has Taken Over

"Remember that all things are a cycle. All moments pass and flow into another. Breathe, focus, and know that you will be okay."

Moma passed away at 3:40 AM on March 11, 2019. She had just had her 89th birthday the day before. I had just left her that evening.

She slipped away gradually, first noticing her lack of engagement during our most recent visits. She would refuse to eat or drink her supplement. She wanted to sleep more and do less. Focus became difficult. She started refusing anything by mouth. Pills were crushed and administered with liquid. It was a very hard time. The day before her birthday she was quite agitated. She told me she wanted to go to Heaven. There was a hole in my heart. All I could do was tell her how much I loved her. The medication finally kicked in and she became relaxed.

I stayed with her while she slept until early morning.

She was very quiet on her birthday. Lying in bed, she seemed at peace with herself. I sat with her, sharing her space, talking and remembering, realizing her time was nearing. Somehow, I understood that God had taken over. I had taken her as far as I could. Moma always said that God is busy. We are to do our best always in helping Him out. Afterwards, you need to lift it up to Him.

God lifted Moma up the very next morning.

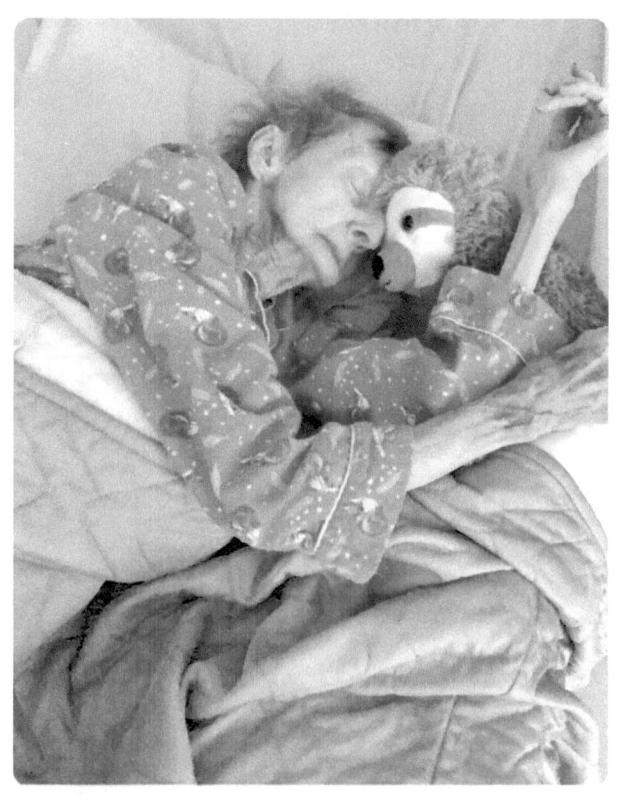

Moma and her sloth.

Sarah

Moma's name was Sarah, with an "h." She was very proud of that h. She told me how she would remind her teachers to put the "chair" at the end of her name. She introduced herself to neighbors as Sarah, with an h. Later in life, she said that the chair had always given her a place of rest along life's passage.

May you always find your chair, Moma.

I Love You Forever

I miss her so. Feelings seem endless. Knowing that she is no longer waiting... waiting for her next journey. Knowing that she is no longer feeling sadness or pain, thank God. Knowing I will never hold her again on Earth—an emptiness inconsolable.

How many times do I forget, for a moment, that I don't need to go see her today? Make her bed. Try to feed her. Do her laundry. There are endless times, only to realize she is with God now.

I have a video that I made of me singing "You Are My Sunshine" to her. She smiles like a child while listening to the words. Her innocence is beautiful. I am glad there were times near the end that she forgot she had dementia. Of course, that means she forgot me too, but it was worth it to see her released from the confusion.

I know she is complete again in Heaven, singing her song and smiling. As my dear friend Jeanne taught me—I am no longer needing to pray for her, but rather to her.

I do so every day.

We had this game we would play. She would say, "I love you." I would say, "I love you more," followed with her saying, "I love you the 'mostest.'" The past few months she changed the last word to "forever."

I take a deep breath and finally exhale. Sadness fills my emotions, yet my consciousness realizes Moma is whole again. She has her mind back. Funny—she would recognize me now. I miss you so much, Moma. I reach for my constant rock, John, to whom I owe so much, as I could not have walked this journey without him.

Moma is now my guardian angel. I carry her in my heart always.

Until we sing again, Moma—
"I love you—
I love you more... I love you, forever."
Atwaba.

www.ingramcontent.com/pod-product-compliance
Lightning Source LLC
Chambersburg PA
CBHW022042290426
44109CB00014B/954